Y0-BQW-775

LEADERSHIP:
A RELEVANT AND
REALISTIC ROLE FOR
PRINCIPALS

Gary M. Crow
L. Joseph Matthews
Lloyd E. McCleary

EYE ON EDUCATION
Suite 106
6 Depot Way West
Larchmont, NY 10538
(914) 833–0551
(914) 833–0761 fax

Copyright © 1996 Eye On Education, Inc.
All Rights Reserved.

For information about permission to reproduce selections from this book,
write: Eye On Education, Permissions Dept., Suite 106, 6 Depot Way West,
Larchmont, NY 10538.

ISBN 1–883001–24–2

Library of Congress Cataloging-in-Publication Data

Crow, Gary Monroe, 1947—
    Leadership : a relevant and realistic role for principals / Gary
M. Crow, L. Joseph Matthews, Lloyd E. McCleary.
      p. cm.
    Includes bibliographical references.
    ISBN 1–883001–24–2
    1. School principals—United States.   2. Educational
leadership—United States I. Matthews, L. Joseph, 1950—
II. McCleary, Lloyd E. (Lloyd Everald), 1924— . III. Title.
LB2831.92.C76 1996
371.2'012—dc20   96–13802
                                             CIP

10 9 8 7 6 5 4 3 2

Editorial and production services provided by Richard H. Adin Freelance
Editorial Services, 9 Orchard Drive, Gardiner, NY 12525 (914-883-5884)

Published by Eye On Education:

Block Scheduling: A Catalyst for Change in High Schools
by Robert Lynn Canady and Michael D. Rettig

Teaching in the Block: Strategies for Engaging Active Learners
edited by Robert Lynn Canady and Michael D. Rettig

Educational Technology: Best Practices from America's Schools
by William C. Bozeman and Donna J. Baumbach

The Educator's Brief Guide to Computers in the Schools
by Eugene F. Provenzo, Jr.

Handbook of Educational Terms and Applications
by Arthur K. Ellis and Jeffrey T. Fouts

Research on Educational Innovations
by Arthur K. Ellis and Jeffrey T. Fouts

Research on School Restructuring
by Arthur K. Ellis and Jeffrey T. Fouts

Hands-on Leadership Tools for Principals
by Ray Calabrese, Gary Short, and Sally Zepeda

The Principal's Edge
by Jack McCall

The Administrator's Guide to School-Community Relations
by George E. Pawlas

Leadership: A Relevant and Realistic Role for Principals
by Gary M. Crow, L. Joseph Matthews, and Lloyd E. McCleary

Organizational Oversight:
Planning and Scheduling for Effectiveness
by David A. Erlandson, Peggy L. Stark, and Sharon M. Ward

Motivating Others: Creating the Conditions
by David P. Thompson

Oral and Nonverbal Expression
by Ivan Muse

The School Portfolio:
A Comprehensive Framework for School Improvement
by Victoria L. Bernhardt

School-to-Work
by Arnold H. Packer and Marion W. Pines

Innovations in Parent and Family Involvement
by William Rioux and Nancy Berla

The Performance Assessment Handbook
Volume 1: Portfolios and Socratic Seminars
by Bil Johnson

The Performance Assessment Handbook
Volume 2: Performances and Exhibitions
by Bil Johnson

Bringing the NCTM Standards to Life
by Lisa B. Owen and Charles E. Lamb

Mathematics the Write Way
by Marilyn S. Neil

Transforming Education Through Total Quality
Management: A Practitioner's Guide
by Franklin P. Schargel

Quality and Education: Critical Linkages
by Betty L. McCormick

The Educator's Guide to Implementing Outcomes
by William J. Smith

Schools for All Learners: Beyond the Bell Curve
by Renfro C. Manning

FOREWORD

The School Leadership Library was designed to show practicing and aspiring principals what they should know and be able to do to be effective leaders of their schools. The books in this series were written to answer the question, "How can we improve our schools by improving the effectiveness of our principals?"

Success in the principalship, like in other professions, requires mastery of a knowledge and skills base. One of the goals of the National Policy Board for Educational Administration (sponsored by NAESP, NASSP, AASA, ASCD, NCPEA, UCEA, and other professional organizations) was to define and organize that knowledge and skill base. The result of our efforts was the development of a set of 21 "domains," building blocks representing the core understandings and capabilities required of successful principals.

The 21 domains of knowledge and skills are organized under four broad areas: Functional, Programmatic, Interpersonal, and Contextual. They are as follows:

FUNCTIONAL DOMAINS
- Leadership
- Information Collection
- Problem Analysis
- Judgment
- Organizational Oversight
- Implementation
- Delegation

PROGRAMMATIC DOMAINS
- Instruction and the Learning Environment
- Curriculum Design
- Student Guidance and Development
- Staff Development
- Measurement and Evaluation
- Resource Allocation

INTERPERSONAL DOMAINS
- Motivating Others
- Interpersonal Sensitivity
- Oral and Nonverbal Expression
- Written Expression

CONTEXTUAL DOMAINS
- Philosophical and Cultural Values
- Legal and Regulatory Applications
- Policy and Political Influences
- Public Relations

These domains are not discrete, separate entities. Rather, they evolved only for the purpose of providing manageable descriptions of essential content and practice so as to better understand the entire complex role of the principalship. Because human behavior comes in "bunches" rather than neat packages, they are also overlapping pieces of a complex puzzle. Consider the domains as converging streams of behavior that spill over one another's banks but that all contribute to the total reservoir of knowledge and skills required of today's principals.

The School Leadership Library was established by General Editors David Erlandson and Al Wilson to provide a broad examination of the content and skills in all of the domains. The authors of each volume in this series offer concrete and realistic illustrations and examples, along with reflective exercises. You will find their work to be of exceptional merit, illustrating with insight the depth and interconnectedness of the domains. This series provides the fullest, most contemporary, and most useful information available for the preparation and professional development of principals.

> Scott D. Thomson
> Executive Secretary
> National Policy Board for
> Educational Administration

If you would like information about how to become a
member of the **School Leadership Library**, please contact:

Eye On Education
Suite 106
6 Depot Way West
Larchmont, NY 10538
(914) 833–0551 Phone
(914) 833–0761 FAX

ABOUT THE AUTHORS

Gary M. Crow, associate professor, educational administration, University of Utah, received his Master of Education degree from Bank Street College and the Doctor of Philosophy degree from the University of Chicago. He served as an early childhood teacher and an administrator in an early childhood program and a secondary alternative school. His publications, including articles, book chapters and monographs, and his conference presentations focus on leadership, the principalship, socialization, and school reform. He has conducted research projects in three U.S. cities, on the subjects of principal internships and socialization.

L. Joseph Matthews, clinical professor in the Department of Educational Administration at the University of Utah, has also served as a high school teacher and a principal of three high schools in Nebraska, Wyoming and Utah. He received his Bachelor of Arts degree from the University of Wyoming, and the Master of Education degree and the Doctor of Education degree from Brigham Young University. He has extensive experience in staff development for principals and was the director of the Utah Principals Academy before his present assignment at the University of Utah. He has written and presented on various topics related to school leadership, namely school choice, site based management, professional practices, reflective decision making and mentoring.

Lloyd E. McCleary, professor emeritus, educational administration, University of Utah, has conducted numerous research projects relating to the principalship, including major U.S. and international studies. He has authored or coauthored 10 books and many articles, monographs and research reports. His educational preparation includes Kansas University, LSU, the Sorbonne, and the University of Illinois where he earned the Doctor of Education degree. He has taught and served as a principal and assistant superintendent in the public schools.

PREFACE

In 1993, the National Policy Board for Educational Administration published a description of the 21 domains of the principalship. These domains identify the body of knowledge and skills that define the field of educational administration. There remains the task of drawing together, in scholarly fashion, the best thinking regarding each of these domains, and this book represents a portion of that task.

The first domain focused on the topic of leadership, which is the subject of this book. The Policy Board and the consultants who developed the domains understood the importance of leadership for the principal's role. The major issue in school improvement today is leadership, whatever image that may conjure. Many reform movements have questioned the relevance of the role of the principal as a leader. The teacher professionalism movement has emphasized the teacher's leadership role in instruction. Some school improvement literature has argued that principals have a useful but not a necessary role to play in innovation projects. These movements leave open the question of whether principal leadership is critical. Fortunately this debate has not stopped effective principals from exercising leadership. Nevertheless, for current and prospective principals the nature of a leadership role that is realistic and relevant is worth consideration.

The topic of leadership for schools is not an easy task to treat. This topic has many facets about which there is genuine disagreement; there are problems that are difficult to research, and some that are not researchable; and the demographic and constantly changing social context requires new interpretation and study. However, much is known that can be of use to those in the principalship and those preparing for it.

In today's schools the principal functions in a context quite different from that of a few years ago. Gary Crow, Joseph

Matthews, and Lloyd McCleary have attempted in this book to define leadership for principals that is both realistic and relevant. This definition recognizes the multiple sources of leadership in the school and fact that principals follow as well a lead, Yet it also acknowledges that a relevant leadership role for principals is still not only possible but critical. The tremendous chance occurring in contemporary schools and the uncertainty of what principals, teachers, students, and parents will face in future schools strongly suggest the need for a critical leadership role for principals.

The authors have aimed this book at both current and prospective principals. Current principals will find it helpful in their role, especially in a changing environment. The self reflection and peer reflection called for in this book are crucial to enable current principals to question whether their assumptions about leadership are relevant for contemporary and future schools and to consider alternative perspectives. Prospective principals will also find the book useful in introducing them to a definition of the principal's leadership role that may be different from what they experienced as teachers. As they prepare to be school administrators, they should consider how leadership is both a realistic and relevant part of their jobs. This book encourages them to do so.

David A. Erlandson
Alfred P. Wilson

ACKNOWLEDGMENTS

Several people have been helpful in bringing this book to publication. We appreciate the work of David Erlandson and Al Wilson, series editors, in encouraging and goading our efforts. Our colleagues at the University of Utah were valuable sources of ideas and support. Kate Rhodes was helpful in organizing and compiling bibliographic information. Ann Hart and Danny Talbot were perceptive and critical reviewers who made significant contributions to whatever thoughtful and clear ideas are found in the book. Finally, our spouses and families were major sources of support for this endeavor. Their love and encouragement enabled us to complete this book.

TABLE OF CONTENTS

1

PRINCIPAL LEADERSHIP: EVERYTHING OR NOTHING

Writings and discussions about principals as leaders tend to identify two extremes. On one extreme, principals are encouraged to be charismatic leaders and sole agents for improving the school's instructional program. This instructional leadership role often assumes a larger than life "lone ranger" or "pied piper" quality. Principals as leaders are expected to construct a vision for the school and inspire others to accept and implement it; they envision and create, singlehandedly, a more effective school.

At the other extreme, principals are admonished to take a less creative approach to leadership, one in which they become facilitators of others' leadership. In this role, principals are expected to be conveners or parliamentarians, bringing teachers, parents, and the community together to decide the vision of the school; they are to be fundraisers, providing resources that enable teachers and other groups to create a more effective school. Although these responsibilities are surely valuable to the school, many principals question whether they involve a significant leadership role.

Neither of these extremes alone—everything or nothing— constitutes a realistic or relevant leadership role for principals. Realistically, leadership in schools cannot be limited to the action of a single individual. For schools to change in substantive ways, leadership must include more than one person and frequently be exercised by those without formal administrative titles. Relevantly, principals can and should inspire others to follow their lead in making schools effective environments for students and adults.

This book is about the leadership of principals. Its purpose is to provide a perspective for defining the principal's leadership role that is both realistic and relevant and to apply that perspective to three areas of school leadership: culture, vision, and change.

This first chapter lays the groundwork for a discussion of this perspective of the principal's leadership role. We begin by asking why leadership is important for principals and then move to a discussion of how principals know about leadership. These two topics will inform the reader of some of the authors' assumptions about leadership that form the basis for the framework that follows in Chapter 2.

WHY IS LEADERSHIP IMPORTANT FOR PRINCIPALS?

Some readers will find it strange to ask this question, since they may argue that leadership has been an important topic for principals for decades. However, the origin of the principalship and its practice until recently have not always emphasized a leadership role for principals. The earliest reason for principals had little to do with leadership and more to do with unlocking the doors and managing the daily routines. Indeed the managerial function of the principalship rather than any leadership qualities has received most of the attention (Beck and Murphy, 1993). Principals were assumed to be more like business executives, using good management and social science research to run schools effectively and efficiently.

In the early 1980s, with the effective schools movement, principals moved to an "instructional leadership" role. Instead of simply managing the operation of the school, principals were expected to inspire and influence students, teachers, and occasionally parents and community members to focus on the instructional environment.

The topic of leadership has grown in importance for contemporary principals and prospective principals because of three sources of leadership: external sources; internal sources; and the principal's own leadership.

LEADERSHIP FROM EXTERNAL SOURCES

New principals quickly discover that school leadership is practiced by individuals and groups outside the school. The principal does not have a monopoly on the practice of leadership.

Other administrators in the school system, in particular board members, the superintendent, and other district officials, exercise leadership by influencing district agendas; recruiting, selecting, and evaluating principals; attending to and rewarding particular administrative behaviors; and focusing community involvement. Schools are nested in districts and therefore are both nurtured and constrained by them. Although site based management in some cases has increased the autonomy of principals and teachers, it has hardly replaced district administrators' leadership and authority.

Government agencies can also provide leadership. For example, state governments have taken a stronger leadership role in education in the past decade (Odden, 1995). Governors, state legislators, and state educational officials exert leadership by focusing public attention on particular features of school effectiveness, by directing the use of public monies for specific instructional uses, and by intensifying the monitoring of school outcomes.

Parents and other community groups also exercise leadership that affects the practice of principal leadership. Parents influence curriculum options, choose schools and occasionally teachers, and provide scarce resources. Other community groups also exercise leadership in schools. Political interest groups, e.g., taxpayer associations and religious organizations, exercise leadership by influencing public opinion to limit public monies to schools, and by staging protests over instructional strategies and curriculum approaches.

Principals work within a context in which leadership is exercised by various external sources. These external leadership sources make it clear that principals are not the sole leaders of schools. However, principals need to recognize leadership coming from these sources and attempt to influence them for the benefit of their schools.

LEADERSHIP FROM INTERNAL SOURCES

Besides the external sources of leadership in schools, teachers, counselors, and students can and should provide leadership. Recent reforms, such as site-based management and restructuring, emphasize stronger leadership roles for these individuals inside the school. These reforms emphasize what has been the case for some time—teachers, counselors, students and others exercise leadership outside of formal role designations. Because of their proximity to students and their potential, if not actual, expertise in curriculum and instruction, teachers are in the most obvious and most effective place to exercise instructional leadership.

Students also play a leadership role in schools. One has only to compare the numbers of students versus staff to understand this group's potential for leadership. Student leadership's potential for good or bad is tremendous and frequently overlooked. The norms and values of leaders within the student body influence the academic and personal behavior of other students.

A realistic leadership role for principals acknowledges the leadership provided by teachers, students, and others. Otherwise, principal leadership in key areas such as culture, vision, and change is unlikely to be effective. The leadership role of principals includes the development of the leadership potential of teachers and students. School leadership is a more potent source for improvement if the leadership of others is developed and used.

PRINCIPAL LEADERSHIP

The topic of leadership is also important because principals need to understand their own leadership practice and development. Knowing how to influence individuals' actions and how to develop others' leadership potential is a significant endeavor. For example, recognizing the limits of formal position as a leadership source is important for principals. As with the junior high administrator discussed in the following illustration, principals can develop the reflective skills to recognize and assess the ways that their experience, intentions, values, and formal training influence their practices (Hart and Bredeson, 1996). They can then identify the leadership that can actually attack a problem or condition. Such reflection increases their potential for effective leadership.

With the help of this book and simple observations and discussions, current and prospective principals can consider their leadership role in realistic and relevant ways—to reflect on what influences and constrains their own leadership and in what ways they can exercise leadership in contemporary schools. Each chapter will conclude with a vignette comparing the leadership reflections of two principals. As we describe a perspective for principal leadership and apply it to three areas of leadership practice, we will use the vignette to ground our discussion and present questions and activities for reflection.

ILLUSTRATION

One principal's first attempt to correct a tardiness problem was to strengthen a policy that she perceived as weak. Mary Cannella, principal of Cloud Crest Middle School, set up a new tardiness policy and with her assistant spent considerable time in the halls trying to enforce it. At first it seemed to help, but Mary found it exhausting and time consuming to be constantly enforcing the tardy rule. The enforcement of the rule fell on the assistant principal and soon tardiness was back to where it was before the new policy.

After considerable reflection, Mary realized that if the leadership for this policy was confined to her, it would never be effective. Without the support and ownership of the teachers, two administrators walking the halls to enforce a tardy rule was not going to work. She began with discussions with student leaders, teacher leaders, and ancillary personnel such as custodians. In this collaborative strategy, larger problems such as student motivation and instructional practices emerged.

HOW DO WE KNOW ABOUT LEADERSHIP?

If leadership is important for school principals, how do they learn about it? In this section, we identify two major sources of knowledge about leadership: its practice and its literature. Both sources are basic to the framework used in the remainder of this book.

LEADERSHIP IN PRACTICE

Principals do not construct their conceptions of leadership in a vacuum. The general society, other principals, the organizations in which they work, and their own experiences influence the ways school administrators understand leadership and develop their own leadership roles.

SOCIETY

How principals imagine what leadership consists of and what leaders are supposed to do is affected by the images they see around them. These images are especially influential in the case of political and military leaders. General Schwarzhopf, who gains media attention by being thrown into the spotlight during a military operation, affects the conception that individual citizens have of how leaders act, how their followers act, and how they influence individuals to accomplish goals. We are impressed with leaders who are larger than life, and we consciously or unconsciously try to imitate the characteristics they exemplify and, in a sense, model for us.

Besides political and military heroes, society influences conceptions of leadership through ideas and images arising in other occupations. For example, business management has been a dominant source of influence on images of educational leadership. Callahan (1962) chronicles the ways in which scientific management had a significant impact on the conduct of educational administrators through business heroes such as Andrew Carnegie, J.P. Morgan, and John Rockefeller. Tyack and Hansot (1982) chart school administration history from the nineteenth century evangelical missionary to the twentieth century scientific manager. It is easy to see parallels between leadership images conceived by business management and those emphasized by preparation and training programs in educational administration, e.g., chief executive officer or facilitator of shared decision making. Not long after business executives became infatuated with Japanese styles of group decision making and work structures, school principals were encouraged to use management teams, focus groups, quality circles, and to become facilitators of shared decision making.

OTHER PRINCIPALS

The general society is only one source for understanding leadership. Principals enter the position with countless hours of observation of other principals. Lortie (1975) estimates that by the time an individual becomes a teacher she has spent 13,000 hours of observation of other teachers—primarily as a student. Although students observe principals far less than teachers, they leave high school with contact with school administrators that exceeds their contact with those in most other professions. With the addition of the time as a teacher, new principals begin their careers as administrators with a significant number and variety of leadership role images. It is certainly a much longer exposure period, although shorter training time than exists for most professions, including law and medicine. Thus, it is not surprising that Greenfield (1977) found that veteran principals were the most significant influence on the socialization of new principals. It is also not surprising to find that this heavy dose of influence by veterans tends to filter out conceptions of leadership considered outrageous or radical by most principals. Preparation programs also contribute to leadership images but far less than this experience with other principals. Recent changes in administrator preparation programs in which clinical components, such as internships, are emphasized may increase the influence of the preparation experience on images of leadership (Murphy, 1993; Milstein, Bobroff, and Restine, 1991).

ORGANIZATION

Until recently the effect of the school where a principal works has been largely ignored as a source of leadership images and a source of influence on the kinds of leadership that can be exercised and by whom. The logic has been that when principals enter a new school, they bring with them qualities of leadership; while these may be affected by organizational conditions, the school has very little impact on leadership behavior. However, literature on leader succession (e.g., Hart, 1993), suggests the contrary. Schools act as socializing agents, not only for newcomers but for veteran principals. Teachers, parents, and students express and reward the types of leadership qualities and images that fit the context and are accepted by constituents. Thus, the images which principals carry with them regarding how leaders behave and how followers respond are partially revised depending on the school context in which they work.

ILLUSTRATION

Linda Morgan, the new principal of Kennedy Elementary School, came to the inner city school from eleven years as a teacher in suburban schools. Soon after arriving she offered to demonstrate a lesson using computers—one of her specialities. Shortly after beginning the lesson, Linda realized she had lost control of the class. The teacher brought the class to order and Linda apologized. Later, she asked the teacher if she could return and try the lesson again. When she returned the next week, she found a group of teachers seated in the rear of the classroom awaiting her "performance." Fortunately, during the week she had reassessed her views of classroom management to more adequately fit her new environment. The lesson was successful and Linda won over not only the students but the teachers who appreciated her humility and her adaptability.

Linda's leadership was tested by the teachers and her image was revised due in part to the reaction of students and teachers in the new school. Fortunately for her, she had good skills of reflection and sensitivity to her environment.

INDIVIDUAL PRINCIPALS

Lest we assume that principals are simply passive recipients of leadership images from society and organizations, we should emphasize that the individual principal influences the leadership image. The personal context, including career stage, life stage, professional experiences, and critical life events, shapes principals' images of leadership (Hart, 1993; Greenfield, 1983). Life and career stage affect the kinds of heroes and leaders that principals select to admire. The situations, events and role models of their past professional experience suggest conceptions of leadership that make sense to them and that serve as models for their own development of a leadership image.

LEADERSHIP LITERATURE

Although practice is a powerful source for understanding leadership, principals—through preparation programs, professional associations, readings and in service education—are exposed to the leadership literature. In this section, we present an abbreviated review of the leadership literature that provides another basis for the framework we will present in the next chapter.

The leadership literature is vast and inconsistent. Chester Barnard, in 1948, said that "leadership has been the subject of an extraordinary amount of dogmatically stated nonsense" (p. 80). Although the body of knowledge of leadership is lacking, there is much that is known and we attempt to provide one way to organize and understand it. Our attempt is not to provide an exhaustive, extensive review of the literature but to offer a description of how this research and theory relate to the leadership role of principals. We begin with a discussion of six major themes in the literature.

Leadership as—

+ A personal quality;
+ A type of behavior;
+ Dependent on the situation;
+ A relationship;
+ An organizational feature; and
+ A moral quality.

LEADERSHIP AS A PERSONAL QUALITY

The oldest and most persistent way of thinking about leadership is as a set of personal qualities that separate leaders from non-leaders. The "great man [sic] theory" of leadership has a long history and persists to this day in everyday conversation. For example, the high school student who is encouraged by adults to take leadership responsibilities is usually described as assertive, persuasive, and an example for other students to follow. Descriptions of principals who are perceived by their teachers to be leaders typically include personal traits, such as future-oriented and decisive. Older versions of this perspective identified physical and personality characteristics, such as height and self-esteem.

The early attempts to identify and measure leadership traits were unsuccessful primarily because of the lack of any evidence that such personal qualities guaranteed leadership effectiveness. When most observers found individuals without these characteristics, who were nevertheless considered leaders, the credibility of the research became suspect. These attempts failed because they ignored the possibility that the relationship between personal qualities and leadership success might be indirect (Yukl, 1994).

Recently, interest in the personal qualities of leadership has been resurrected as social scientists acknowledge that other factors may intervene between personal qualities and leadership effectiveness (Yukl, 1994). For example, such factors as school context and teacher influence, while not eradicating the effect of the personal qualities of the principal, nevertheless intervene in the relationship with leadership success.

In addition, recent literature has expanded the types of personal qualities associated with leadership. Qualities such as energy level and stress tolerance (Howard and Bray, 1988), emotional maturity (McCauley and Lombardo, 1990), and achievement orientation (Stahl, 1983) have been identified and studied for their effect on leadership success and group performance. Baltzel and Dentler (1983) found that the recruitment and selection of school principals still rely on certain personal qualities, notably those that enable the principal to "fit" with other district or school features. Thus, while there are difficulties in defining leadership as personal qualities, the common sense notion that leaders have traits that nonleaders do not possess is alive and well.

LEADERSHIP AS A TYPE OF BEHAVIOR OR ACTIVITY

When early trait theory did not adequately account for differences between leaders and non-leaders, social scientists began to look at what leaders did. The famous Ohio State University studies on leadership identified two major factors of leadership behavior: initiating structure (task orientation) and consideration (person orientation) to categorize leadership behavior. Leadership was defined as what leaders did to move the organization toward the achievement of goals and to motivate and inspire followers to contribute to this achievement. Thousands of research articles and dissertations, many of them concerning the principalship, have used the Leadership Behavior Description Questionnaire (Stogdill, Goode, and Day, 1962), which categorized behavior as initiating structure or consideration.

Simultaneous with the Ohio State studies, investigators at the University of Michigan examined differences between effective and ineffective leaders (Likert, 1961, 1967). These studies, like the Ohio State research, examined managers and assumed that leadership qualities would be found in them. The Michigan studies identified three types of leadership behavior that differentiated effective and ineffective managers: task-oriented, relationship-oriented, and participative. The Ohio and Michigan studies agreed on the two major types of leader behavior, task and person, found in effective managers. Principals displaying task orientation focused on such behaviors as planning, monitoring, and coordinating school processes, while principals displaying person orientation focused on such behavior as informing teachers of decisions and praising their accomplishments.

Early research based on these behaviors attempted to develop prescriptions for how leaders behaved, whatever the situation. They argued that exemplary leaders always balanced high task orientation and high person orientation behaviors. Others argued that the balance depended on other intervening features such as context and follower characteristics (Blake and Mouton, 1982). These situational influences on leaders' behaviors led to a third perspective.

LEADERSHIP AS DEPENDENT ON THE SITUATION

The situational perspective added maturity to leadership literature by identifying some intervening factors that influence leadership behavior and effectiveness. Principals become successful leaders not only because they behave in certain ways but because these behaviors are affected by school characteristics. Among these contextual factors are teacher effort and commitment, teacher ability and role clarity, cooperation and teamwork, organization of work and performance strategies for it, resources needed to do the work, and external coordination (Yukl, 1994).

Fiedler (1964, 1967) identified a contextual variable, situational favorability, that intervenes between leader behavior and effectiveness. Favorability depends on three factors: leader-member relations, position power (i.e., the leader's authority to evaluate and to distribute rewards and sanctions), and task structure (i.e., the degree to which the job has objective procedures for accomplishing it). Thus, principal behavior should influence effectiveness depending on the relationship between the principal and teachers, the degree to which the district grants the principal discretion in evaluating and rewarding teachers, and the objectivity of the specific teaching tasks that the principal is evaluating.

Other school characteristics may intervene between principal leadership and issues of school effectiveness. For example, Rowan and Denk (1984) found that students' socioeconomic backgrounds influenced the effect of the principal's leadership on student achievement. Principals' leadership had more effect in schools where there was a high percentage of students of low socioeconomic status.

Besides the situational characteristics that influence leaders' behavior and its effectiveness, there are factors that substitute for or neutralize the effect of leaders. Kerr and Jermier (1978) and Pitner (1986) identified substitutes that take the place of leadership behavior. Kerr and Jermier identified three types of substitutes or neutralizers: subordinate characteristics (e.g., experience, training or, value of rewards for subordinates), task characteristics (e.g., routine, structured, or unambiguous tasks), and organizational characteristics (e.g., a cohesive work group).

LEADERSHIP AS A RELATIONSHIP

The move from the leader's personal qualities to situational constraints acknowledged that followers matter. What should have been obvious—leadership cannot exist without "followership"—was largely ignored in these earlier perspectives. The situational or contingency theories finally acknowledged that follower characteristics, primarily those inherent in the organizational or group context (e.g., experience, training, and effort), influence leadership effectiveness. Yet they ignored the influence that followers themselves have on the leader.

Leadership as a relationship grows out of social science literature, particularly from political science, that emphasizes power and influence. This perspective began by focusing on the leader's influence or power over the follower. The approach identified the types of power that leaders use with followers, for example, position power (control over resources and rewards) versus personal power (expertise and charisma) (French and Raven, 1959; Yukl and Falbe, 1990). The leadership as relationship perspective also described the kinds of influence tactics used by leaders, including rational persuasion, inspirational appeals, consultation, ingratiation, personal appeals, exchange, coalition tactics, legitimating tactics, and pressure (Yukl, 1994). Although informative as to how leaders influence followers, this literature ignored the reciprocal nature of the leadership relationship.

When the follower's influence on leaders is taken seriously, the identification of leadership tactics and power resources becomes more relevant. For example, Blase (1989) identified nine tactics that teachers use to influence principals, including diplomacy, conformity, extra work, visibility, avoidance, ingratiation, documentation, intermediaries, and threats. The reciprocal nature of this influence is reflected in Blase's finding that the proportion of influence tactics used by teachers depended in part on the principal's political orientation, either open or closed. Whether a principal was open or closed depended on such factors as expectations, communication, collegiality, and support. Teachers working with open principals were more likely than those working with closed principals to use diplomacy, extra work and visibility.

This perspective also encourages a consideration of how external sources influence the leadership relationship. Events, situations, agencies, and individuals create opportunities and constraints that affect the balance of influence and power in the leadership relationship. For example, the succession of principals in a school affects the personal and formal power of both teachers and principals (Hart, 1993). Also, government regulations and district mandates noticeably affect the leadership relationship in a school by promoting or limiting the autonomy of principals (Crow, 1990).

LEADERSHIP AS AN ORGANIZATIONAL FEATURE

The emphasis on followers' influence broadened the attention of leadership literature beyond the formal leader. Another perspective, leadership as an organizational quality, raised this attention to another level. Moving beyond defining leadership as particular roles, leadership as an organizational quality focuses on the social interaction among roles in the organization. This perspective has roots in the work of several organizational theorists, including Barnard (1938), Thompson (1967), Katz and Kahn (1966), and Tannenbaum (1962).

More recently, Ogawa and Bossert (1995) describe leadership as an organizational quality in schools from an institutional theory viewpoint. They identify the purpose, nature, context, and medium of leadership. Instead of the traditional emphasis on leadership to accomplish organizational goals, this perspective focuses on leadership as helping to legitimate the organization's existence and survival, to encourage its acceptance by various constituents. As to its nature, leadership as an organizational quality emphasizes the relationship among roles. Ogawa and Bossert illustrate this social network in schools and school districts by identifying the resources of knowledge possessed by individuals in different school system roles.

> In school organizations, district superintendents use their knowledge of state guidelines to influence school boards, principals and teachers. Principals employ their knowledge of budgets to influence the decisions of both district superintendents and teachers on school councils. Also, teachers use their knowledge of effective instructional techniques to affect principals and district curriculum directors (1995, p. 235).

According to Ogawa and Bossert, the context of leadership is the culture of the organization. Leadership as an organizational quality involves attempts to shape organizational culture, including its norms, values, and beliefs. Finally, the medium of leadership, according to this perspective, includes the traits and actions of individuals within their roles as they socially interact. In this way traits and actions go beyond characterizing individuals and provide the resources used to influence others.

This perspective is particularly useful in understanding school leadership by broadening our understanding of leadership beyond one role or position to acknowledge the interaction among roles for the occasion of leadership. In this way principals' actions and traits can be described in terms of leadership without assuming they are sufficient for leadership to occur in the school.

LEADERSHIP AS A MORAL QUALITY

Thus far the leadership perspectives we have examined are nonevaluative. They could be used to describe Hitler as well as Gandhi, Attila the Hun, or Omar Bradley. They involve transactions between and among followers and leaders to achieve some task, to support certain types of behavior, to overcome some situational constraint, or to influence some activity. Yet they do not account for the occurrences of leadership to transform organizations. Burns (1978) defines transformative leadership as a process in which "leaders and followers raise one another to higher levels of morality and motivation" (p. 20).

The previous perspectives tend to focus attention on the self interests of followers and leaders to accomplish some task to receive reward, or to realize some individual or organizational objective. However, leadership as a moral quality goes beyond these simple exchange transactions, to raise consciousness to higher levels, even to question individual or organizational objectives. This allows leaders and followers to evaluate the direction of their organization and to work together to achieve some greater purpose. Gardner (1965) relates this view to societal leadership. Leaders "express the values that hold society together. Most important, they can conceive and articulate goals that lift people out of their petty preoccupations, carry them above the conflicts that tear a society apart, and unite them in the pursuit of objectives worthy of their best efforts" (p. 12).

Burns' (1978) notion of *transformational leadership* has recently gained attention in the educational leadership literature. Leithwood and his colleagues at the Ontario Institute for Studies in Education (Leithwood and Jantzi, 1990; Leithwood and Steinbach, 1991, 1993; Leithwood, 1994) have applied the notion of transformational leadership to the work of principals. They identify various transformational leadership practices of principals as to purpose (e.g., builds a consensus about school goals and priorities); people (e.g., provides intellectual stimulation); structure (e.g., distributes the responsibility and power of leadership widely throughout the school); and culture (e.g., uses symbols and rituals to express cultural values).

As this last set of leadership practices suggest, the work on leadership as a moral or transformational quality also produces an interest in the symbolic or cultural side of leadership (Schein, 1992). Whereas most leadership work has focused on the technical side of leadership, be it task- or person-oriented, this perspective focuses on the values, beliefs, and assumptions of work—how values and beliefs are formed, how they affect the quality of life and work in schools, and how they are modified. Leadership from this perspective examines what principals do to build and maintain a school culture that reinforces values, norms, and beliefs and to add meaning to educational work that goes beyond mere accomplishment of discrete tasks.

CONTROVERSIES IN THE LITERATURE

This review of the leadership literature identifies at least three controversies that have engaged writers and researchers. These controversies also influence our attempt to develop a framework for understanding and redefining the principal's leadership role that is realistic and relevant.

First, there is a controversy between those who view leadership as an individual property and those who view it as part of a social system (Yukl, 1994). The common way to see leadership is as a feature of individuals. The latter view, however, sees leadership as a feature of a social system, for example, a classroom or school, where both leaders and followers participate in leadership and where a particular individual or role is less important than the interaction and relationship between individuals and roles.

Understanding leadership as an individual feature naturally leads to a singular focus on leaders' behaviors. When leadership is the same as what leaders are and do, there is a tendency to ignore what followers do and the important role they play in the process of leadership. Rost (1991) suggests that the leadership literature of the 1980s in particular has intensified this way of understanding leadership.

> Taking its cue from the past, the 1980s saw leadership recast as great men and women with certain preferred traits influencing followers to do what the leaders wish in order to achieve group/organizational goals that reflect excellence defined as some kind of higher-level effectiveness (p. 91).

If we make the principal into the sole agent of school leadership, we ignore the multifaceted nature of the school and environmental situations in which principals find themselves. Although in this book we concentrate on leadership from the principal's perspective, we attempt to do so without assuming that school leadership is solely what principals do.

The second controversy lies in distinguishing leadership and management. Some writers argue that leadership must be distinguished from management since it is possible for someone to be an effective manager without leading (Zalesnik, 1989). Likewise, one can be a leader, e.g., of an informal group, without having managerial responsibilities or authority. However, the difficulty arises not so much in denying they are the same thing, as in describing and delineating those areas in which they overlap. Can a principal be an effective leader without being a good manager, i.e., making sure the organization runs smoothly? Leithwood (1994) found that it is not so easy to distinguish leadership and management based on examining the overt behavior of principals. Rather, transformational leadership involves "school leaders infusing day-to-day routines with meaning and purpose for themselves and their colleagues" (p. 515).

Rost (1991) suggests that blending leadership and management runs the risk of labeling anything leadership. This can be seen in current restructuring literature where the act of facilitating teachers' work, e.g., obtaining resources, is considered leadership. Yet facilitation, or any other managerial activity, is not leadership unless, as Burns (1978) and Leithwood (1994) have suggested, it is infused with educational meaning and purpose. Leadership may begin with management but it does not end there. In our discussion of the principal's leadership role we will focus on leadership rather than management but acknowledge that at times managerial practice can be used as a leadership resource.

The third controversy, according to Yukl (1994), is which influence processes count as leadership. For some writers, only those processes related to task objectives or group maintenance can count as appropriate leadership processes. For others, any attempt to influence may count as leadership. Murphy (1988), in a survey of the instructional leadership literature, suggests that too often we narrowly define what counts as instructional leadership and ignore behaviors such as indirect activities, symbolic and cultural activities, established organizational activities that act as substitutes for leadership, and organizational routines infused with educational meaning.

A leadership role for principals that is relevant and realistic does not appear out of thin air. Rather, such a leadership role evolves from the practice and literature of decades and the circumstances of contemporary schools. The leadership role that individual principals develop will be influenced by these factors. In this book, we attempt to aid current and prospective principals in shaping their leadership role in relevant and realistic ways.

FORMAT OF BOOK

This chapter has provided the groundwork for an identification and discussion of a framework for the principal's leadership role. Chapter 2 presents this framework examining the nature, participants, location, purposes, and methods of leadership from the perspective of the principal.

In Chapters 3 through 5, we apply this framework to three key concerns of principals as leaders. Chapter 3 examines how principals exercise leadership in creating, maintaining, and shaping school culture and values. Chapter 4 focuses upon the principal's leadership role in influencing a collective vision. Chapter 5 turns to a realistic and relevant leadership role for principals in school improvement and change. Each of these chapters will use the vignette introduced below and subsequent additions to illustrate the specific leadership issues and pose questions and activities for reflection.

The final chapter provides a summary of our examination of leadership from the principal's perspective and describes future trends that may impact principal leadership.

REFLECTIVE VIGNETTE

The following vignette describes two principals, their contexts, and the beginnings of their reflections on their leadership roles. Following the vignette, we offer three sets of questions and activities to aid current and prospective principals in reflecting on a leadership role in light of the issues raised in the chapter. The first set of questions is designed to aid current and prospective principals in analyzing their own leadership roles. The second set is designed for groups of current and prospective principals as they work among themselves in reflecting on leadership practice. Finally, we offer a set of course activities to be used in preparation or inservice programs to stimulate discussions of the principal's leadership role.

Flight 465 to New Orleans was taxiing out on the runway at its scheduled time of 9:40 a.m. Richard Gonzales sat in his window seat staring outside as the crews of various airlines scattered around jet liners. The captain came on over the intercom and announced that due to heavy traffic, their flight to New Orleans was going to be delayed. His last words were, "Sit back and relax and we will be on our way soon." Richard sighed, thinking about the statement "sit back and relax." That is just what he needed: time to sit back and relax. If it's on a plane sitting on the runway, fine. He was going to the annual ASCD conference and he was hoping the time away would be relaxing, refreshing and invigorating.

His schedule lately had been more than just hectic, not as it once was before all of the changes at school. As principal of Meadowlark Elementary School, he had little time now to sit back and relax. This past year Meadowlark had changed into a year-round schedule due to increased enrollment in the suburb. Considerable anxiety was associated with the change as many parents and teachers complained about the new schedule and the disruption it had caused in their lives. Although it was a district decision, Richard took on the leadership of implementation and, therefore, the brunt of the complaints. At first he, too, wasn't in favor of the change. He could not understand why the district wanted to make changes in a school that was doing so well. Meadowlark had consistently ranked at average to above average on the state test for the past ten years. He thought the district could bus the kids to less populated schools rather than impose a year round schedule onto Meadowlark.

Richard had gradually accepted the need for the year round schedule but he had no idea it was going to be so time consuming. He had decided to visit every neighborhood and have evening cottage meetings. He empathized with many parents, understanding how disruptive a different schedule would be for some families. Nevertheless, he continued meeting with the community to get their ideas, and hopefully, their support. He worked with the teachers, organizing them into teams to share in the implementation. It was exhausting work and now that it was finished, he was looking forward to getting away for a few days and attending this conference.

Among other pressing matters, Richard had been aware of a petition being circulated around the community asking for the removal of three new teachers at Meadowlark Elementary who were recently hired to fill the additional faculty needs for the year round schedule. Fortunately, the petition had gone nowhere and he thought it was a dead issue now. Nevertheless, he became aware that he was going to have to exert some leadership and either help these three new teachers improve or begin a termination process. He hated the very thought of firings. He knew how divisive a termination would be with the faculty.

Seated next to Richard was Carolyn Duncan, principal of Central High, an inner city school. Carolyn was also going to the ASCD conference in New Orleans although neither knew the other nor their destination. Carolyn was obviously uptight as she heard the captain's message about waiting on the runway. The last thing she wanted was to sit in a plane. She was meeting an old friend of hers at a quaint little restaurant in Jackson Square. If this plane is late, it would throw her whole schedule off. She pulled out her laptop computer and began working on a grant proposal. She hoped this proposal would turn into $50,000 in technology money available from the state.

As Carolyn opened the file with the proposal, she began reading the information. One of the grant's requirements was for a site-based decision-making committee. She paused and thought about that. The high school had no such committee and she was not sure how to go about getting such a team together. The faculty at the high school did not volunteer for such things. Most teachers felt that they had enough on their plates to teach these inner city kids, let alone try to take on any more work. They often met anything Carolyn tried to initiate with skepticism.

Her sigh at thinking about it gave Richard an excuse to break the ice. "Going to N'Orlins for business or pleasure?"

"Both," she replied. "I have a conference to attend but also a friend to visit. I also want to sit in my hotel room and get caught up on some work. That is why I brought this li'l babe along," pointing to her Toshiba.

The thought went through his mind that he was seated beside a heavy-duty business exec.: probably a finance analyst judging from the suit she was wearing and the work she was doing. He thought about his own days as an insurance executive. It was good work, good salary, but he never liked the routine work involved. He had been a junior high school social studies teacher but left teaching and took up insurance work for more money. Richard had regretted the move and finally went back to graduate school and pursued his master's degree in educational administration. Richard continued the conversation: "No heavy work for me. I hope I can leave my work and my worries behind on this trip."

Carolyn looked up from her laptop and gave Richard a quick lookover. He was dressed casually, wearing Levis, a sport shirt, and Nike tennis shoes. His sunglasses were hanging from a blue Chub around his neck.

Carolyn returned to her proposal, trying to decide how best to create a decision-making team at her school so she could satisfy the requirement of the grant. She decided that she would insert the names of the department chairs and use them as the team. Each of the chairpersons was getting a stipend anyway, and she could persuade each to come to a few meetings a year so they could fulfill this requirement. She knew some would resist, but then that was the way it usually was. She had decided sometime ago that certain things were best for the school and so she kept pushing for new things to be happening.

Her mind drifted for a moment as she thought about her upcoming dinner engagement with Florence Hyatt. Florence was one of the most remarkable people Carolyn had known in her career. She had met Florence at the University when she was doing her graduate work. Florence was an adjunct professor who came on campus once a week and taught a school leadership course in the program. She was a practicing administrator in the central office. She and Carolyn had developed a good friendship over the semester and she had turned out to be a true mentor for Carolyn. There were too few school leaders such as Florence. She had been one of the first women in a Midwestern state to become a high school principal. She then moved to the central office after being a principal for nineteen years. Carolyn wanted to be known in her state as a true educational leader, much as she perceived Florence was known. Carolyn had landed this innercity high school, and it was a giant step for her and for the board to appoint her. She had been the second female that the board had appointed to an innercity high school. She had been told to "clean it up" and that was exactly what she was trying to do. She wanted so much to talk to Florence about it all and could hardly wait for their evening together. "If only this stupid plane would take off," she thought.

No sooner had she thoughtfully made that request than the plane started to move. The captain came over the intercom and informed the crew and passengers that they had been given clearance for departure. This broke the meditating of both Carolyn and Richard. They were looking out the window when Richard asked about her line of business.

SELF-REFLECTION ACTIVITIES

♦   Chapter 1 describes leadership from external and internal sources. Reflect on these sources that affect the leadership found in Richard and Carolyn's schools. What external and internal sources are affecting your school or district?

+ We learn a lot about leadership from other leaders. How does Carolyn's role model, Florence Hyatt, affect her career and her leadership? What role models have helped you develop a leadership image?

+ Burns (1978) defines transformational leadership as a process in which "leaders and followers raise one another to higher levels of morality and motivation" (p. 20). What experience have you had with leaders who you felt were transformational? What has facilitated and impeded your ability to be a transformational leader?

PEER-REFLECTION ACTIVITIES

+ Principals understand that other individuals and groups, besides the principal, exert leadership. Identify both internal and external individuals and groups that are affecting leadership in Richard and Carolyn's schools?

+ With a peer describe the influence that other principals have had on your view about school leadership.

+ Some people hold heroic images of leaders. With a peer reflect on your observations of how heroic images influence leadership practice.

COURSE ACTIVITIES

+ Chapter 1 identifies two major sources of knowledge about leadership: practice and literature. In the vignette, Richard and Carolyn are influenced by societal, organizational, and individual forces. Find evidence of each and be prepared to discuss your findings in class. Also describe forces that have influenced your knowledge about leadership.

+ Send class representatives to a local book store to investigate the kinds of leadership literature that exist and report their findings to the class. As a class discuss the positive and negative effects of these sources of literature on school leadership.

- In a class discussion, reflect on the positive and negative influences that business management has had on school leadership practice?

- Some argue that principals do not have to come out of the academic ranks but could be selected from business, military or other public sectors. As a class, debate this issue.

- Blase (1989) identified nine tactics that teachers use to influence principals: diplomacy, conformity, extra work, visibility, avoidance, ingratiation, documentation, intermediaries, and threats. In a class discussion relate illustrations of each of these nine tactics.

- Divide into two groups. Using Burns' definition of transformational leadership, students in one group discuss those external and internal forces that *promote* transformational leadership; students in the second group discuss those external and internal forces that *impede* transformational leadership.

2

A FRAMEWORK FOR PRINCIPAL LEADERSHIP

In Chapter 1, we acknowledged the need to avoid all-or-nothing definitions of principals' leadership roles by defining leadership in both relevant and realistic terms. This means taking seriously the complex environments in which principals work and the important role they have to play in contemporary schools. In this chapter, we present a framework for principal leadership that attempts to accomplish this.

This framework is organized in terms of five features of leadership applied to the principal's role: nature, participants, location, purpose and methods. We examine each topic as preparation for our application of the framework in Chapters 3 through 5.

THE NATURE OF LEADERSHIP

Earlier we identified three controversies in the leadership literature: leadership versus management; leadership versus leaders; and leadership as an influence relationship. The following discussion of the nature of leadership responds to these controversies.

LEADERSHIP IS NOT MANAGEMENT

First, we focus on leadership and distinguish it from management. This is not to suggest that management in schools is less important or even less desirable than leadership; management and leadership are different. Management is clearly a responsibility of school principals. However, principals in a leadership relationship do something beyond management; they influence others. Planning, coordinating, and monitoring are important management tasks, but they are different from inspiring, guiding, and persuading. Basically, leadership is concerned with influencing while management is concerned with directing.

Rost (1991) defines management as "an authority relationship between at least one manager and one subordinate who coordinate their activities to produce and sell particular goods and/or services" (p. 145). Whereas management is a relationship based on authority, leadership is a relationship based on influence. Formal position may be a resource used to influence others but it is certainly not a necessary condition of leadership. "Bosses are not necessarily good leaders, subordinates are not necessarily effective followers. Many bosses couldn't lead a horse to water. Many subordinates couldn't follow a parade. Some people avoid either role. Others accept the role thrust upon them and perform it badly" (Kelley, 1992, p. 143).

Leadership and management *can* be related. Leaders may use managerial activities to influence others. For example, a principal may attempt to persuade others to follow some direction by intentionally coordinating activities in a way congruent with her vision. By infusing managerial activities with attempts to influence others toward some purpose, they may become leadership activities. However, the relationship between management and leadership is neither necessary nor sufficient.

LEADERSHIP IS NOT LEADERS

Although our focus in this book is certainly on principals, we understand the leadership relationship as consisting of more than the activity of one individual or position. Schools are complex environments that are more likely to change and adapt because of interrelationships rather than the inspiration of one individual.

By focusing on leadership rather than leaders, we avoid the trap of defining principal leadership solely as a set of traits or personal qualities. Although in our discussion of leadership we will describe actions, qualities, and mental images of principals, these have relevance for leadership only within an influence relationship in which principals may be leaders or followers at different times.

LEADERSHIP IS AN INFLUENCE RELATIONSHIP

Our framework of leadership is based in part on Rost's (1991) definition of leadership as "an influence relationship among leaders and followers who intend real changes that reflect their mutual purposes" (p. 102). In this section we will emphasize the "influence relationship" and turn to the role of leaders and followers and also the purpose of the relationship in later sections of this chapter.

For a relationship to involve leadership it must not be coercive (Rost, 1991). Although management relationships can be based on coercion, leadership relationships cannot. They must be entered freely by both leaders and followers. Influence attempts can result in three possible outcomes: commitment, compliance, and resistance (Yukl, 1994). Commitment occurs when an individual wholeheartedly approves of the decision or request and internalizes the purpose of the decision. Compliance occurs when the individual agrees to the request but without any enthusiastic support. Resistance occurs when the individual opposes the request or disagrees with the decision. All three outcomes must be possible if the leadership relationship is noncoercive. When principals attempt to persuade teachers of the value of collaboration, this attempt may constitute leadership only if teachers perceive they have the choice of committing to the idea, complying with it, or rejecting it.

Those participating in a leadership relationship use a variety of "power resources" to persuade others. These may include expertise, position, reasoned argument, reputation, prestige, personality, purpose, status, content of the message, interpersonal and group skills, give-and-take behaviors, authority or lack of it, symbolic interaction, perception, motivation, gender, race, religion, and choices (Rost, 1991, p. 105). "Influence does not come out of thin air. It comes from leaders and followers using power resources to persuade" (Rost, 1991, p. 160). Principals frequently use a combination of power resources to persuade the district to accept the school's agenda, e.g., reasoned argument, give-and-take behavior, and personality.

ILLUSTRATION

John Blake, principal of Hillcrest Elementary, describes the struggle to persuade district administrators to allow kindergarten through second grade teachers to drop letter grades. At first, the Assistant Superintendent for Curriculum responded that this would create complaints from parents and was not possible unless all schools were given this option. But John and the teachers at Hillcrest kept up their struggle, defending their position with research on authentic assessment. In addition, they convinced several vocal parents to support their argument. At last, district officials gave permission to pilot the idea for two years.

John and the Hillcrest teachers, by using reasoned argument and political clout, influenced the views of district administrators.

In Chapter 1, we reported Blase's (1989) research on the tactics used by teachers to influence their principals. Blase's investigations emphasize the micro political nature of school organizations (Bacharach and Lawler, 1980; Hoyle, 1986; Ball, 1987). Instead of the unidirectional influence assumed by some studies and even in popular descriptions of the principal's role, teachers and principals are in an exchange relationship where both parties are attempting to influence each other. This does not mean that the power resources or influence tactics are evenly distributed or used. Typically there is an unequal distribution of resources that enables one party to be more powerful in the leadership relationship. In schools, principals frequently have more resources to use in influencing school constituents, e.g., position and rewards. However, any veteran principal would acknowledge that teachers, parents, students and community members have power resources that they use to influence each other and the principal.

THE PARTICIPANTS IN A LEADERSHIP RELATIONSHIP

Leadership, as an influence relationship, assumes the presence of both leaders and followers. These designations are not based on formal position or authority. Persons without formal position exert leadership every day in schools. For example, the parent whose political clout influences actions by school staff and the student whose persuasiveness and popularity affect classroom dynamics both exert leadership.

ILLUSTRATION

Recently the Green Valley School District constructed a new middle school. The boundaries for attendance areas for the existing and new middle school had to be drawn. Though the district received public input, a parent enlisted the support of other parents in a neighborhood to challenge the board's decision. Eventually, the board had to recognize the support of this parent and conceded to collect more information. Ultimately they changed their original plan for attendance areas. Considerable effort, by both the board and the parent group, was made to collect data, arouse parent, teacher and student interest, and to present alternative solutions. However, the leadership effort of this one parent was highly influential in the final discussions.

Inherent in the meaning of leadership is followership. There are no leaders without followers. But the role for followers is not the passive role sometimes assumed. In leadership as an influence relationship, followers play an active role.

Kelley (1992) identifies three categories of skills and characteristics possessed by exemplary followers in formal organizations, which suggest followers' active roles. First, these followers prove their value to the organization. They accomplish this by how they perform their jobs, by being focused and committed to organizational goals, and by taking initiative to increase their value to the organization. Second, followers weave a web of relationships in the organization by working with teams, networks and leaders. These relationships intensify their value to the organization and their work effectiveness. Third, exemplary followers exhibit a courageous conscience. They are willing and able to disagree with directions the leader has chosen if they feel they are inappropriate. Exemplary followers actively attempt to persuade leaders at times to change course or direction.

Followers, and leaders, use power resources or influence tactics to persuade each other of certain directions. Implicit in Kelley's three roles of followers are such power resources as expertise, interpersonal and group skills, reasoned argument, and purpose. Although there is frequently an inequality in the influence relationship, both leaders and followers attempt to influence each other. In the vignette at the end of Chapter 1, Carolyn Duncan tends to act in aggressive ways. Yet her teachers have obviously influenced her to avoid innovative practices that might demand more of their time.

Not only are followers active, but the designations of leader and follower are not permanent designations. They change at different times in different contexts. In the same school, an individual may be a leader around one issue or direction and a follower in another. The principal may be a leader in one situation and a follower in another. For example, teacher expertise in the use of technology in the classroom sometimes surpasses that of principals. Good principals will encourage these teachers to lead the school in technological innovations.

This more dynamic sharing feature makes leadership a community endeavor. As Foster (1989) remarks,

> The idea that leadership occurs within a community suggests that ultimately leadership resides in the community itself. To further differentiate leadership from management, we could suggest that leadership is a communal relationship, that is, one that occurs within a community of believers. Leadership, then, is not a function of position but rather represents a conjunction of ideas where leadership is shared and transferred between leaders and followers, each only a temporary designation. Indeed history will identify an individual as the leader, but in reality the job is one in which various members

of the community contribute. Leaders and followers become interchangeable. (p. 49)

The perspective taken in this book is that of leadership from the principal's viewpoint. This does not mean that only principals are leaders or that principals never follow the lead of teachers, students, parents, or community members. The examination undertaken here, however, focuses on the principal's perspectives, actions, and qualities within a leadership relationship.

THE PRINCIPAL AS LEADER OF LEADERS

The school principal is one leader in a context of leadership—a "leader of leaders" (Schlechty, 1990). Schlechty's phrase grows out of his and others' (Senge, 1990) argument that organizations in the future must be knowledge-work organizations focused on organizational learning. Instead of the traditional hierarchical arrangement where decisions are made at the top and passed down, the entire organization must contribute to the problem solving, information processing responsibilities. In this kind of school, students, teachers and administrators have different roles. Students become workers and customers, actively participating in the construction of knowledge. Teachers "become both inventors and leaders" (Schlechty, 1990, p. 43). And principals become leaders of leaders, who are "creators of conditions in which other leaders thrive, and developers of leaders. . . . (They) cause others to decide, they orchestrate, they coach and encourage" (pp. 43–44). And we would add, they inspire and persuade others to follow some direction.

Instead of school leadership being isolated and limited to one position or individual, leadership is more pervasive and systemic (Crow and Slater, 1996). Influence relationships are being developed and pursued at classroom, school, and community levels, involving different school constituents. We can, then, identify leadership roles for both principals and others in the school. For purposes of illustration we discuss the leadership roles of teachers and principals. By doing so we reject the idea that other staff, parents, community members, and even students do not exert leadership. Rather we want to illustrate that principals are leaders of leaders.

LEADERSHIP ROLES OF TEACHERS

Teachers play both leading and following roles in a leadership relationship. First, they directly provide leadership by influencing each other to adopt particular views of the school's purpose, culture, and improvement efforts. They use instructional expertise, experience, charisma, interpersonal skills, political clout, and countless other "power resources," to influence their colleagues. The teacher professionalism reforms of the past few years remind us of the expertise that teachers bring that can be used in reforming schools (Lieberman and Miller, 1991).

Teachers also directly influence principals by taking the lead in various curriculum reforms and working condition improvements. They negotiate, create successes that reflect well on the principal, and use other influence tactics to secure the resources they need and further the purposes they consider important (Blase, 1989).

ILLUSTRATION

A music teacher at Frederick Douglas Elementary School influenced her principal to develop a program in which all elementary students in this inner city school would play a stringed instrument. She reasoned that such a program could bring pride to the school, as well as student and parent involvement in a cultural activity. The principal's first reaction emphasized consideration of costs, scheduling, space availability, and student/parent interest. But, with the principal's permission, the teacher wrote a grant and received funding for a pilot project. The first year's success convinced the principal of the value of the project. In its third year of implementation, the school has received regional and national attention for the program.

But teachers also play a follower role influencing the principal to take on particular leadership roles that contribute to the vision, culture, and school improvement strategies to which teachers are willing to commit. Teachers display followership by both overt and subtle responses. Their statements and behavior encourage leadership images they believe are most appropriate and acceptable for principals to adopt. The literature on change clearly reminds us of how teachers revise and restructure change mandates at the classroom level (Berman and McLaughlin, 1978; Lieberman and Miler, 1991). Teachers use subtle ways of influencing principals in the leadership relationship, e.g., halfheartedly responding to particular initiatives. They also influence principals by the way they do their jobs to add value to the organization, the relationships they form, and their courage to disagree (Kelley, 1992).

LEADERSHIP ROLES OF PRINCIPALS

Principals in turn also play both leader and follower roles in the leadership relationship. Principals influence teachers to buy into a vision, a set of values and beliefs, and change efforts that the principal may author. Using such power resources as rewards, charisma, and expertise to influence teachers in these areas of school improvement, the principal can play a significant instructional role.

Principals also exert leadership in developing and supporting the leadership of teachers and school constituents. Developing leadership potential, far from taking away from the principal's leadership role, adds to it by increasing the overall leadership resources to realize the school's vision, change the culture, and improve the instructional program.

But principals also play follower roles overlooked in the past. An important area for followership is the principal's response to teachers' visions and ideas for improving the school's instructional program. By respecting and encouraging these visions and modeling behavior that facilitates the accomplishment of these purposes, principals are exhibiting follower behaviors. This type of followership influences teachers to risk constructing and communicating a vision with their colleagues. By exhibiting follower behavior, principals can influence teachers to lead in collaborating and experimenting with new school improvement models.

Principals are both enactors and encouragers. As enactors, they influence others to accept approaches to culture development, vision formulation, and school improvement. As encouragers, they champion the leadership behaviors of teachers and others in the school in creating change.

This makes principal leadership both realistic and relevant. It is realistic because schools are complex organizations where leadership must come from more than one individual or more than one position in order for change to occur. It is relevant because the influence occurs both by being a follower and a leader—thus increasing the leadership resources and power aimed at achieving school goals.

ILLUSTRATION

Peter Lucke, an elementary principal in the southern part of the U.S., exemplifies this followership behavior. Peter supports the leadership role of teachers in the school in several obvious ways. For example, he backs the Accelerated Schools inquiry strategy used by the school, by which teachers, parents, and administrators identify major school-wide problems, examine alternative strategies for solving these problems, and attempt to influence each other to accept particular strategies.

But Peter also influences the leadership of teachers by respecting this inquiry/approval process even when it means submitting his own proposals to staff inquiry and approval. This not only shows his commitment to the Accelerated Schools process but proves his faith in the leadership of the teachers—a major and profound act of following.

THE LOCATION OF LEADERSHIP

Most descriptions of the principal's job have focused exclusively on the school site. Principals are responsible for managing and leading teachers and students at the school. This view of the principal's role ignores the nested nature of school organizations, especially concerning the central office and the expanded nature of that role in systemic reforms.

Studies of the relationship between the school and central office, raise apparent contradictions. Several investigations found little overt influence of the central office on the school (Hannaway and Sproull, 1978). Other studies, however, identified ways in which the district affects school instructional decisions (Gamoran and Dreeben, 1986). Investigations of principals' perceptions of the district's involvement in their work demonstrate the presence of supervision, control, and influence (Peterson, 1984; Crow, 1990). Finding principals who complain that central office negatively influences their relationships with teachers is not difficult. They say district administrators influence these relationships by refusing to treat the school site as unique, by putting principals in untenable positions, by creating chaos with district decisions, and by reducing the principal's autonomy (Crow, 1990). In our first segment of the vignette, Richard Gonzales felt this frustration when the district forced Meadowlark Elementary into a year-round schedule. Teachers complained about the disruption this schedule created for them.

The primary adult influence relationship within the school is between principals and teachers. When central office limits the principal's autonomy, it reduces the power resources that the principal can use to influence teachers. This effect is especially critical in site-based management situations where influence relationships between principals and teachers (in both directions) are crucial for the effective work of the school.

But the principal's influence goes beyond teachers and students. With such school change strategies as interagency collaboration, school choice, and systemic reform, the principal's leadership role is enlarged beyond both the school and district office (Murphy and Hallinger, 1993). Principals are involved with governmental units, nongovernmental agencies, and business partnerships. The role of the principal in these contexts requires the principal to be more than head of the school or middle manager, by moving to the roles of entrepreneur and symbol manager (Crow, 1992). As entrepreneurs, principals are responsible for marketing the school's vision to outside constituents who provide resources and support for the school. Hallinger and Hausman (1993) found that principals in schools of choice were more likely to see themselves as entrepreneurs and to spend more time outside the school. As symbol managers, principals are responsible for leading those inside and outside the school to develop and maintain the symbols, norms, and values of the school.

When Richard Gonzales, in the vignette, began his career as a principal he was probably less concerned about parent involvement than he was later as he steered his elementary school into a year-round schedule. A decade or two ago he thought the school was more an extension of the state and decisions could be more or less mandated for the good of the cause. Veteran principals such as Richard are first to say that working with the community is far more of a leadership strategy than it was when they began their careers.

Our view of the location of the principal's leadership is systemic. No longer can the principal exercise leadership totally within the school. Leadership must be exerted throughout the larger educational system. To describe this view of the leadership relationship, we examine both internal and external features of the principal's leadership role.

INTERNAL SPHERE OF LEADERSHIP

Although the principal's leadership role has been enlarged to include people and agencies outside the school, the primary responsibility is at the school site. Internally, the leadership relationship involves teachers, students, administrators and parents. All these individuals are included in the leadership relationship, i.e., they are leaders and followers, actively attempting to influence each other.

To illustrate the internal sphere of leadership, we use three key areas on which leadership is focused: (1) school culture; (2) vision; and (3) school improvement (Thomson, 1993). Although the remainder of this book focuses on these three areas, we briefly describe each at this point.

Creating, maintaining, and changing school culture involves the development and reinforcement of beliefs and norms that govern the behavior of the community within the school. Leaders and followers attempt to influence each other regarding which norms and values are considered most appropriate, given the purpose and mission of the school. For example, teachers or administrators try to influence others to accept such norms as collegiality and experimentation (Little, 1982), and to value those practices that benefit students. As we will see in Chapter 3, the principal usually inherits a culture that must be reinforced and sometimes changed to respond to internal and external conditions.

Influencing a collective vision involves "creating and gaining commitments to broad, long-range visions for the school" (Thomson, 1993, p. 1.5). This collective vision must include the mutual purposes of both leaders and followers. If it is only the leader's vision, it is not shared. The vision is developed by negotiation, compromise, and the use of other power resources as teachers, students, parents, and administrators work out their own views of the school in ways that are acceptable to others.

Influencing school improvement efforts involves the development of an environment for change supported by school constituents. Again if the strategies to develop this environment are only the leader's—no matter whether that is the principal or teacher—they will not encourage community effort and commitment. The leadership relationship requires that both leaders and followers help set goals and develop strategies to meet these goals.

EXTERNAL SPHERE OF LEADERSHIP

The principal's leadership role involves external constituents as well in a systemic view of leadership. Principals must become involved at the state and national government levels, in community agencies, and the district office. To illustrate the external sphere of leadership, we again use the three features of culture, vision, and school improvement.

Creating, reinforcing, and changing school culture becomes crucial in a systemic context in which external constituents must know not only what the mission of the school is but the culture and set of values behind this mission. Principals who fail to communicate adequately their school's culture and values abdicate leadership and run the risk of external constituents confusing the school's purposes. However, communicating school culture and values also includes sensitivity to the issues raised by external constituents in the influence process by which culture is formed and values are prioritized.

Influencing collective vision involves expressing the vision and purpose of the school to outside constituents and, by that, encouraging their contributions to the accomplishment of this purpose. But this external role also involves addressing concerns regarding purpose identified by external constituents as they and school staff negotiate a shared vision.

Influencing school improvement involves identifying external constituents who can provide resources to aid in school improvement efforts. In order for this to happen, principals must ensure that culture building and collective vision are addressed. Before external constituents can understand and support school improvement efforts, they must understand the school's culture, values, and vision. But they must have an opportunity to influence the environment for school improvement.

The dilemma for principals in a systemic context of leadership is one of balancing—balancing internal norms, vision, and strategies with external demands. If leadership is multidirectional, principals must expect that external constituents will attempt to persuade as well as be persuaded.

THE PURPOSE OF LEADERSHIP

Couldn't schools exist without formal leaders? If principals were excellent managers who kept the organization running smoothly, finding resources for teachers and balancing task and people concerns, wouldn't that be enough?

But most people want to believe in the value of school leadership. To argue for the value of leadership means adding a purpose to our influence relationship. What are leaders and followers trying to accomplish through influencing each other?

LEADERSHIP FOR CHANGE

Leaders and followers attempt to influence each other in order to "intend real change based on mutual purposes" (Rost, 1991). The purpose of leadership involves the intention to change the organization in substantive ways.

The basis of the change lies in the mutual purposes of leaders and followers. We depict leadership primarily from the perspective of the leader who develops a vision or purpose for the organization and convinces followers to accept this vision. But, as we have stated earlier, leadership involves active followers and leaders. From this perspective, leadership must intend change based on the shared purposes of both leaders and followers. The influence relationship involves negotiation and compromise leading to the development of these shared purposes.

ILLUSTRATION

In one of the classic case studies of educational administration (Gabarro, 1974), David King became principal of Robert F. Kennedy High School. He inherited a situation in which a school, designed to be innovative and based on the "house concept," was in the throes of major internal conflict among the administrators regarding the school's vision. Some administrators contacted the media to criticize the school, others threatened to resign, and others threatened each other to stay out of their buildings.

A typical response of educational administration students to the conflict in this case is for principal King to create order by fiat. Yet King had a wealth of expertise and commitment among the staff that could contribute to a renewed sense of shared purpose and thus to the leadership relationship.

Leadership is important in the Kennedy School and other schools because of the need for leaders and followers to come together around some change that is based on their mutual purposes. Leadership, as we will see in a following chapter, becomes important in helping individuals define their purpose and develop a collective vision for the school.

Leaders and followers also inspire each other to evaluate their mutual purposes. If we stop at intending change based on mutual purposes, we risk ignoring those situations in which we should evaluate and revise our purposes for the school. We also risk "groupthink," where like-minded individuals ignore any critical element that should be introduced into their conversation. The idea of transformational leadership suggests that we move beyond mere transaction to consciousness-raising where leaders and followers together critically assess their purposes in light of the school's situation (Burns, 1978).

THE METHODS OF LEADERSHIP

In our framework for leadership, we have discussed the nature, participants, location, and purpose of leadership. We now turn to the methods. Obviously in remaining chapters we will focus in more detail on how leadership is practiced, but some general comments about the methods of leadership are in order at this point to understand how a realistic and relevant leadership role is practiced.

THREE AREAS OF LEADERSHIP

In Chapters 3 through 5 we apply our leadership framework to three areas of principal practice: culture, vision, and school improvement (Thomson, 1993). This is not to suggest that these are the only leadership areas pertinent to principals, but rather they are used to illustrate how principal leadership is practiced in ways that are realistic and relevant.

The influence relationship is especially pertinent in these three areas. In the culture area, leaders and followers influence each other as they create, maintain, and change norms and values that govern their lives together in school. This is clearly a community endeavor and involves mutual persuasion by both leaders and followers. Vision also involves mutual influence as both leaders and followers attempt to persuade each other to develop a collective vision. School improvement is based on leaders and followers developing an environment for change in the school according to the collective vision they have developed within the norms and values of the school's culture. As we mentioned, these functions are performed systemically—that is, both internally and externally.

In the leadership relationships involved in these three major areas, principals use both technical and symbolic methods.

THE TECHNICAL METHODS OF LEADERSHIP

By technical methods, we mean the task- and person-oriented behaviors and processes emphasized in earlier leadership work. Leaders and followers influence each other by their expertise and reasoned argument aimed at accomplishing goals and by their charisma and interpersonal skills used to inspire each other. It is not surprising that we are willing to follow someone who impresses us with their task directedness, their goal orientation, and their exceptional people skills. What makes these behaviors leadership, however, is how they are used in the influence relationship. If no attempt to influence is made, these behaviors become good management, but not leadership.

Robert E. Lee, the Confederate general, possessed the skill of a strategic planner as well as the ability to influence his troops. In spite of the ultimate military defeat, Lee developed the reputation with both friends and enemies as an astute, technical leader.

Deal and Peterson (1994) identify eight ways principals enact leadership that are technical in orientation: (1) planner, (2) resource allocator, (3) coordinator, (4) supervisor, (5) disseminator of information, (6) jurist, (7) gatekeeper, and (8) analyst (p. 19). From our perspective, these functions can be described in terms of an influence relationship. Principals may disseminate information, for example, as a way to influence others. The importance and value of information as a power resource is critical for shared decision making as an educational reform. The capabilities of acquiring valuable information and knowing how to disseminate it strategically and clearly enable the principal not only to influence others to a particular picture of the school's reality but to support teachers as school leaders. The same can be said for each of these technical functions. As they are used as power resources in an influence relationship, they become ways for leaders and followers to exercise leadership.

THE SYMBOLIC METHODS OF LEADERSHIP

Equally important are the symbolic tools used to influence leaders and followers. Starratt (1993) talks about the "drama" of leadership. Duke (1986) describes the "aesthetics" of leadership.

Both emphasize the symbolic tools that are obvious in leadership relationships but seldom attended to in research and training.

John Kennedy's leadership is frequently described in terms of the use of symbolic tools to create an image of Camelot. The appointment of young zealots, the choice of entertainers at the White House, and the phrases and metaphors used in speeches all symbolized a new age.

As they did with the technical forms of the principal's leadership, Deal and Peterson (1994) also identify symbolic forms: (1) historian, (2) anthropological detective, (3) visionary, (4) symbol, (5) potter, (6) poet, (7) actor, and (8) healer. The principal as poet suggests ways in which the principal puts into words the values, norms, beliefs, anxieties, and hopes of followers. These are also power resources used to influence others by means of the vividness and relevance of the description of the school and its environment. The ways principals describe their schools to both internal and external constituents and portray their hopes and values act as powerful tools of persuasion.

> Leaders tend to be those whose reflexive monitoring of the reproduction of social institutions become both more intentional and more abstract. That is, leaders may be the ones, or the group which, through greater concentration on the monitoring of system reproduction, understand how things work, and are in a position to explore imaginatively how things might work better.... Leaders have a larger intuition of the whole institution as a unity, as well as how the parts of the institution work. They may therefore be able to imagine other abstractions of the institution working in different, more effective, or more satisfying ways (Starratt, 1993, p. 39).

SUMMARY

Instead of depicting leadership as management or as synonymous with leader, we have portrayed it as an influence relationship practiced systemically by both leaders and followers for changing schools. This type of leadership is not only possible for principals but vital for our schools. Leadership as an influence relationship acknowledges that principals are "leaders of leaders" rather than sole leaders in the school and that they are both leaders and followers in ways that are critical to the accomplishment of the school's purpose. In this way, principals can develop a leadership role that is both relevant and realistic.

REFLECTIVE VIGNETTE

"Anything here to drink?" the flight attendant asked Richard and Carolyn. Both ordered a diet soda and then resumed their conversation. Ever since the flight had departed and they had found out that they were comrades on the same crusade, their discussion of various issues had not ceased. It was fascinating to Richard that Carolyn had so much energy and that it mostly was directed toward her school and career. He admired her enthusiasm. He had to admit that his approach to this whole school leadership business was more on the side of building relationships with his faculty and staff.

Carolyn, in turn, was impressed with Richard's relaxed disposition. She liked his friendly and open personality. He had nothing to hide. There were no facades. He had told her all about his initial displeasure with the district office administrators imposing the year-round schedule on his school. She had related to it all, since she too often felt imposed upon by the central office.

Carolyn described the proposal she was writing and the difficulty she was having with one teacher in particular. He was a veteran teacher who had considerable influence with the faculty. He was an advocate for teacher rights and benefits. He was also involved in technology and knew more than anyone else in the school about computers and software. She originally had asked him to help her write the grant but their views about the grant were different. In his opinion, every teacher should have a computer. He felt this should be a top priority, even above computer labs and multiple computers in a few classrooms. Carolyn's view was that the kids should have access to the computers and they should have top priority.

She wanted to write the grant to get money for setting up a computer lab for at risk students so they could use it during school and even after school hours. She felt that many at risk kids were turned off with traditional teaching approaches and would turn on to working on the curriculum with a computer. Apparently, they were definitely at odds, so she finally decided she didn't need his help and would write the grant herself.

Richard could detect the disgust that Carolyn had with this teacher. Richard's mind trailed off to his school back home. He had to admit one thing to himself: he liked the people with whom he worked. They were all good to him. In a way, they were all one big family and they looked after each other. The recent changes at the school had not altered the relationships that existed there. Even yesterday, as he prepared to leave for home and finish packing for this trip, the fifth grade teachers brought him a tourist book entitled *Enjoying New Orleans Night Life*. They all laughed about his going and having a party down there. It was all in good fun, and he was feeling a slight bit of guilt that he was going and they all now were in school working.

Carolyn had continued talking and he tuned back into her conversation. Her last comment had aroused his interest. She had stated something around the fact that she wanted to be a strong leader and not just a manager of the school plant. She felt that many of the faculty wanted her to ease off and not exert so much "leadership." He wondered, "What does my faculty think of me? Do they think of me only as a manager of the office or do they think of me as an educational leader? Or better still, are the teachers developing into leaders themselves, or do they rely on me to fulfill that role?"

With that an incident came to mind that helped him answer his own question. Last year when he had gone to a state workshop for a few days, the fifth grade classes had taken a field trip to the local quarry. While on the field trip, a terrible crisis had occurred. One of the three classes had left the group and had started playing on a pile of ore. The kids evidently were climbing the hill and then running back down it. For some unknown reason, the conveyor belt had started and the kids who were on top had been buried with ore. Luckily, the teachers quickly rescued all the children but not until there was widespread panic with the rest of the students and teachers. One teacher, in fact, had become so excited that she collapsed. She had to be taken in an ambulance with the two more seriously injured students. For a while there was chaos with no one exerting any leadership until a plant supervisor emerged. It was an ugly scene, and Richard heard about it from the plant supervisor, the teachers, and the parents. Richard thought that the teachers needed to have shown more leadership in this incident. They should have recognized the harm and avoided it. If the kids did get involved in an unsafe situation, then someone needed to have them stop. Furthermore, he thought that the teachers should have led the group toward the goal of learning about the quarry and the plant operation rather than allowing them to have the field trip be a recreational activity.

Richard had recognized from the field trip incident that this faculty needed more of a sense of leadership. The teachers were mostly young, energetic, and enthusiastic but did not see themselves as leaders.

SELF-REFLECTION ACTIVITIES

♦ Speculate on the type of power resources you think Carolyn and Richard tend to use to influence others.

♦ What power resources do you use most frequently? What power resources do you use least frequently?

♦ Both Richard and Carolyn wish to exert leadership in developing and supporting the leadership of teachers in their schools. What suggestions would you give to Richard and Carolyn to help them develop the leadership potential of their teachers?

PEER-REFLECTION ACTIVITIES

♦ Identify persons whom you have known in education who did not hold official administrative positions, yet were considered leaders by others. Reflect on the kinds of influence they exerted.

♦ With your peer, visit retired or veteran principals. Ask them to describe the leadership role of their first principalship. With your peer, discuss how the leadership role of principals has changed.

♦ Many principals complain about the central office's influence. Reflect on ways the central office exerts influence on you.

COURSE ACTIVITIES

♦ Inherent in leadership is followership. In a class discussion, determine the characteristics of the followers who have affected the leadership of the two principals in the vignette. What characteristics of followers have affected the leadership in your school?

♦ Solicit examples from the class of the leading and following roles that teachers play in schools.

♦ Find a recent job listing or job description for a school administrative position. Identify those qualifications and characteristics that address management responsibilities and those that address leadership responsibilities.

♦ Principals influence others by being enactors and encouragers. Which role best characterizes Richard and Carolyn's leadership behaviors? Support your answer with examples from the vignette.

3

LEADERSHIP AND SCHOOL CULTURE: CREATING, MAINTAINING, AND CHANGING

School culture is the "glue" that holds the school together and that blends the efforts of teachers, students, parents, and administrators toward making a particular type of school. But cultures do not develop full blown, nor are they maintained without effort nor changed without anxiety. A school's culture is pervasive in determining how teachers, students, parents and others view the school, shape their attitudes and their relationships to others associated with it, and conduct themselves in working with others in the school. Therefore, leadership is critical in *creation* of a school culture, *maintenance* of it as a source of stability and predictability, and *change,* where such change can improve school life and effectiveness.

In this chapter, we discuss the role of leadership in creating, maintaining and changing school culture. But before we examine these three features of school culture, we will define culture and its features.

DEFINING CULTURE

Cultures arise as schools attempt to solve two major problems: *external adaptation,* i.e., responding to the demands of the external environment, and *internal integration,* i.e., blending the efforts of individuals inside the school so that there is a coherent set of behaviors (Schein, 1992). Over time, a culture is created: "a pattern of shared basic assumptions that the group learned as it solved its problems of external adaptation and internal integration, that has worked well enough to be considered valid, and therefore, to be taught to new members as the correct way to perceive, think, and feel in relation to these problems" (Schein, 1992, p. 12). Administrators, teachers, students, and parents come to accept certain ways of addressing external demands and develop particular patterns and reasons for behaving. School culture is not something mandated; rather it is constructed by teachers, administrators, students, and parents in ways that enable them to make sense of the school's predictable and unpredictable features. Each school culture is unique and is taught to newcomers as the way "we do things here."

We can think of school culture as consisting of three parts (Schein, 1992; Ott, 1989): artifacts and behavior norms; values and beliefs; and basic assumptions. Artifacts include such features as jargon, metaphors, myths, stories, heroes, ceremonies, rites, and rituals used by teachers, students, administrators, and parents to describe, understand, and replicate school behavior and norms. Values and beliefs of a school's culture provide the reasons people behave as they do and influence the artifacts and norms. Assumptions provide the underlying basis for our actions, beliefs, and values. As school culture becomes embedded, these assumptions are rarely acknowledged.

Culture is an important factor in the stability and effectiveness of schools. School culture is necessary for the school to maintain a sense of "oneness" in the way individuals behave and believe in the organization.

The stability and tenacity of school cultures are often seen by school leaders who make a difference while they are there; but whose vision is more their personal property than the organization's. Therefore, soon after the leader leaves, the school reverts to its old culture. The vision dies with the leader. Commitment is short termed at best and the culture is not altered significantly. Many schools have seen a principal hired to "clean up" or to get a sense of discipline back into the organization.

The principal can, in fact, clean up but then after the initial cleaning up, struggles to capture another cause.

We now turn to a discussion of the three components of creation, maintenance, and change of school culture and treat them in terms of the principal leadership framework described in Chapter 2: nature, participants, location, purpose, and method. As we do so, we attempt to provide both a realistic and relevant view of leadership from the principal's perspective.

THE NATURE OF LEADERSHIP FOR CULTURE

In Chapter 2 we argued that leadership is not synonymous with leaders. Likewise, when we discuss principals' leadership responsibility for the creation, maintenance and change of culture, we are not calling the principal the sole author of the school's norms, beliefs and values. Though, as we will see, this may be the case in creating a culture. The word "culture" suggests a shared process by which norms, beliefs and values develop as individuals work together.

We asserted that leadership is not management. While managerial practices, such as facilitating communication, are important for school culture, they do not constitute the influence relationship of leadership. In this chapter we focus on leadership and culture. "If one wishes to distinguish leadership from management or administration, one can argue that leaders create and change cultures, while managers and administrators live within them" (Schein, 1992, p. 5).

CREATING CULTURE

Although several sources of organizational culture exist, by far the most discussed source is the founder(s). "Founders and other dominant, early organizational leaders seek out and attract people who share their views, values, beliefs, and assumptions and, through the force of their personalities, further shape the culture" (Ott, 1989, p. 81). While creating culture, leaders establish a set of values, beliefs, and assumptions and inspire followers to live by them. If the assumptions turn out to be wrong, i.e., they do not enable followers to make sense of their work, the group fails (Schein, 1992). If the assumptions are right, a powerful culture develops.

Principals are seldom the founders of a school, creating a new culture. Most principals inherit a school with an embedded culture and their role becomes one of maintaining or changing the culture. Nevertheless, with new models of schools being developed, e.g., charter schools and schools of choice, it is not atypical to find a principal in a founder's role, responsible for helping to create a school culture. In these cases, the types of teachers and students recruited, the particular features of school life to which the principal pays attention, and the ways they react to crises help to create an organizational culture.

ILLUSTRATION

An alternative school in Provo, Utah, is aptly named Independence High School. The school is housed in a new building, has a dynamic principal and faculty, and strong academic and work-to-study programs.

Greg Hudnall, principal of Independence High School, helped create a school that serves at-risk adolescents who have consistently failed at the traditional high schools. Greg's leadership role is one of founder and visionary. He was instrumental in raising enough funds from outside sources to help the school district construct the building. Greg works diligently in fusing the curriculum with a culture of caring. Although these at-risk students have often failed in the traditional high school setting, at Independence High School they have had more success. The school meets the individual students' needs through rigorous curriculum and instructional programs, work-to-study programs, and individual and family counseling programs.

As Greg recruits and selects faculty and staff, he specifically looks for individuals with nurturing, caring and tolerant personalities who also have strong instructional skills. The school values and beliefs are permeated throughout the school and even reflected in the school name.

Principals attempt to influence teachers, students, and parents, persuading them that the assumptions on which the school is built are correct and will provide meaning to teaching and learning. Recruiting, hiring, attending to, rewarding, providing resources, and modeling serve as "power resources" for influencing others to embrace a set of norms, values, beliefs, and assumptions.

MAINTAINING CULTURE

Once teachers, administrators, students, and parents agree that the assumptions, values and beliefs are successful in solving the school's internal and external problems, the leadership role of the principal moves to maintaining this culture. This role of maintaining culture involves three audiences: internal veterans, internal newcomers, and external constituents. Leaders maintain culture by influencing those individuals who are veteran group members to "keep the faith"—abide by the norms of the school's culture. Leaders use rituals, ceremonies, stories, and other artifacts to reinforce the values, beliefs, and assumptions of the shared culture.

The second audience to which principals as leaders address the maintenance of school culture are newcomers. The leader's role involves socializing new members to the norms, values, beliefs, and assumptions of the school's culture. This occurs first through the recruitment and selection of teachers who already possess some values and beliefs held sacred by the school. In the previous example, principal Hudnall must continue to recruit and select teachers who reflect the culture of Independence High School.

Yet the socialization also occurs after entry to the school by using artifacts, i.e., stories, rituals, ceremonies, language, etc. Understanding the socialization process of newcomers helps us to understand the culture's features transmitted to them. However, what new members are taught are only surface aspects of the culture. "The heart of a culture . . . will only be revealed to members as they gain permanent status and are allowed to enter the inner circle of the group, where group secrets are shared" (Schein, 1992, p. 13). A major complaint of new teachers is their difficulty in uncovering the "secrets" of how things are done in the school.

The third audience to which leaders must attend in maintaining the culture is external—those individuals outside the organization who are nevertheless related to it. This may include central office administrators, government officials, community leaders and political interest groups. The principal is responsible for communicating the norms, values, beliefs, and assumptions of the school's culture to these individuals and groups to ensure their understanding of and enlist their support for the meaning behind the school's activities. This becomes especially important when external constituents change, e.g., a new superintendent, new government officials, or a new, highly-visible, political group.

CHANGING CULTURE

In addition to creating and maintaining culture, leadership involves changing culture. The two major reasons why cultures need to change reflect the two primary organizational problems: external adaptation and internal integration. First, when environmental demands on the school change and the school's culture is out of step with these demands, cultural change is necessary. "Internal dissent can be forgiven, but a leader who fails in the external functions is abandoned, voted out, or gotten rid of in a more dramatic way" (Schein, 1992, p. 69). The external environment confronting contemporary schools is an excellent example. This environment has undergone rapid and fundamental change in terms of student population, technology, and democratization (Odden, 1995). Thus, principals and teachers struggle with cultural assumptions about student learning and school governance.

ILLUSTRATION

Marsha Lowe, principal of East Madison High School, found herself between two groups of angry parents. In the fall of 1994, Marsha was approached by a parent of an eleventh grader who was upset over the use of the book, *Catcher in the Rye*, in an American Literature class. She discussed the district's policy regarding controversial material with the parent and suggested she complete the request for reconsideration of instructional material. A committee, appointed by Marsha and made up of teachers, parents, and one student, considered the request and narrowly voted to prohibit the use of the book in literature classes.

Marsha thought the situation was settled until another parent found out from her daughter that the book was banned. The parent notified the editor of the local newspaper who wrote a scathing editorial charging censorship in the schools. This parent also filed a reconsideration request and Marsha set up another committee to reexamine the issue. At the next PTA meeting, there was a larger than usual turnout and Marsha encountered two vocal and opposing groups of parents, both sides angry at her.

Eventually the new committee overturned the first committee's ban. The opposing forces have created unrest in the school and threaten the school's previous excellent reputation in the community.

Changing culture also becomes necessary when internal integration breaks down, for example, when morale is low or when individuals perceive that power is distributed unfairly. When groups within the school hold different and opposing values and beliefs, there is little sense of shared community. In these instances, principals must use their influence with followers to reinforce the current set of values or perhaps support cultural change.

ILLUSTRATION

Many schools have attempted to adopt the site-based approach to school governance. Horizon Elementary School faculty concluded that although they valued participation in decision making, they preferred the more traditional approach. Principal Tom Ashby had been with the school for 12 years and had hired most of the faculty. This faculty had developed confidence in Tom and his style of decision making.

They decided that the site-based approach of having to attend team meetings and play considerably more politics in decision-making, distracted them from their work with students. They also felt that it disrupted the interpersonal relationships with their colleagues which were a major part of their school culture. This governance method was abandoned and they are currently looking at other strategies for shared decision making that are congruent with their particular cultural norms.

THE PARTICIPANTS OF LEADERSHIP AND CULTURE

Both leaders and followers play critical, active roles in influencing the creation, maintenance, and change of culture. In creating culture, leaders are probably more influential than at almost any other time. The values, beliefs, and assumptions they hold become the values, beliefs, and assumptions that form the basis of the school's culture. We usually think of principals as fulfilling this leadership role because of their formal position. Occasions when teachers, individually or as a group, work with the principal to establish schools and create organizational culture are more frequent.

ILLUSTRATION

Central Park East Secondary School in New York City was founded by a group of teachers who shared common values and beliefs about student learning, teaching and school governance. They developed these understandings from long association and intense discussions. They came to believe strongly about their work and about their relationship with each other. Although one of the teachers, Deborah Meier, ultimately became the principal and spokesperson for the school, the school's cultural norms and values clearly were created by the teacher group.

Followers play an active role as well in the creating phase of culture development. Their commitment to the values and beliefs provide the opportunity to test these to decide if they work in the internal and external environments of the organization. Without followers' willingness to commit to and live with these assumptions, there is no way to decide if the assumptions are successful.

In maintaining school culture, leaders are responsible for reinforcing and transmitting cultural values and beliefs to group members. Leaders reinforce, socialize and communicate values, beliefs and norms to the three audiences we identified in the last section. In schools, both principals and teachers may serve these leadership functions. For example, when new teachers arrive, the principal may provide the more prominent aspects of socialization, i.e., the norms of conduct. Yet the veteran teachers are more likely to socialize newcomers to the nuances of norms especially regarding expectations about student behavior, innovation, and other areas of teaching practice.

Followers serve at least two major roles in maintaining culture. Their continued commitment to the values and norms are critical for the preservation of the culture. In addition, they become more influential regarding the cultural norms, values and beliefs. This is especially evident when a new principal arrives who is not steeped in the school's culture. Followers in this context are especially skillful in socializing the new administrator to the culture. This can be accomplished through various socialization tactics (Hart, 1993), e.g., withholding information to make the principal more dependent on the assumptions, values, and beliefs of teachers.

Leaders and followers also play crucial roles in changing culture. Leaders are responsible for being sensitive to the ways in which the school's culture does or does not develop successful patterns of behavior and values/beliefs that respond to environmental changes. Moreover, leaders are responsible for recognizing internal integration problems, such as low morale. When either external or internal problems exist, leaders must present the situation to followers in convincing ways that help them acknowledge the problem and must create an environment that eases their willingness to change.

However, leaders are frequently trapped by their own organizational culture (Ott, 1989). This is especially true if leaders were founders and/or have been deeply embedded in the culture for some time. At this point followers can signal leaders that the organizational culture is dysfunctional and change is needed. Frequently a follower or group of followers moves to a leadership position to reinforce and encourage change.

PRINCIPAL AS LEADER OF LEADERS

Besides the obvious roles in creating, maintaining, and changing culture, principals serve a more general cultural role as leader of leaders. This has the qualities we identified in Chapter 2, e.g., encouraging and supporting teachers to take on school leadership roles, especially cultural leadership. First, teachers reinforce with each other and with newcomers the values, beliefs, and norms that are the organization's culture. Second, they act as checks against the principal's own susceptibility to being trapped by the culture. Often they can be the "loyal opposition" (Sergiovanni, 1995), constantly reminding and prodding the principal to be critical of the culture-environment connection. Principals need to support the leadership role of teachers to create and maintain a vibrant culture.

In the vignette presented in Chapter 2, Richard Gonzales's problem with his teachers refusing to accept leadership during the field trip mishap illustrates one reason for supporting the development of teacher leadership. His teachers were unsure how to decide and when to take authority.

The principal's role as leader of leaders also has a symbolic and cultural function, which is typically ignored. "Managers, to be effective . . . must attend to the celebration of their own existence. They must properly dramatize their own role. This is a difficult point in American culture, with its exaggerated emphasis on action and decision and its inattention to constitutive existence. The manager is supposed to do something. But the point here is that the manager is supposed to be" (Meyer, 1984, pp. 201-202).

In another illustration, one author learned the lesson of this symbolic role the hard way. He sent his assistant principal to the annual athletic banquet in place of himself. The resulting comments and complaints from parents and teachers let him know: no one but the principal would do. The principal served as the symbolic head of the school. Expectations became widely shared that the principal's presence was a symbol of the importance of athletic activities.

THE LOCATION OF LEADERSHIP FOR CULTURE DEVELOPMENT

The two problems of external adaptation and internal integration emphasize the spheres in which principal leadership occurs in developing school culture. Rather than the principal demonstrating leadership only inside the school, it is critical that leadership is demonstrated to external audiences as well.

When internal integration breaks down, e.g., when staff have very little sense of shared purpose, leadership is necessary either to reinforce the current culture or to lead the school to change the culture. The principal's leadership role becomes one of analyzing the current culture, and helping to develop new norms, rules, languages, and reward systems that reflect a different set of assumptions, or reinforcing the current norms, rules, languages, and reward systems that have been ignored. The principal's role also involves working with teachers and students to soften the anxiety produced by change, recalling them to traditional values and beliefs, or influencing them to consider the need for a new set of norms, values, and beliefs.

The principal's external leadership role has at least two components. First, the principal must sensitively address environmental concerns and demands. Because the environment of the school is becoming more complex and the rate of change is accelerating, principals cannot afford to ignore environmental concerns regarding what schools should be and provide for the environment. Ignoring the changing nature of the world in which students live and will work is a certain route to loss of school resources and legitimacy. Principals as leaders serve a critical role by understanding the reality, expressing the concerns, and influencing teachers and students to join in finding appropriate ways to address these concerns.

The other component of the principal's external leadership role is to communicate to the district office and the community the values, beliefs, and assumptions the school has developed in response to environmental issues, and to persuade these constituents of the values' appropriateness. Most school communities are too complex and heterogeneous for principals to respond uncritically to environmental demands. The principal's leadership role involves critically analyzing the environment's concerns, leading the school in determining in what ways the organization's culture must adapt, and persuading environmental groups to accept the school's values and beliefs. Leadership in schools must acknowledge the critical role environments play but not abdicate moral responsibility for critically assessing their demands.

ILLUSTRATION

Post (1992) describes schools in a district outside Los Angeles where there had been a large migration of families seeking schools more closely aligned with their "traditional" values. A new social studies curriculum, emphasizing multicultural education, was introduced. The ensuing controversy pitted the old-timers who supported the new curriculum against the newcomers who objected to it.

Instead of a homogeneous parent population, principals and central administrators were confronted with conflicting values and beliefs and resulting demands. These administrators found it necessary to critically assess the demands of a diverse population rather than to uncritically concede.

THE PURPOSE OF LEADERSHIP FOR CULTURE

In Chapter 2, we maintained that the purpose of leadership is to "intend real change based on mutual purposes" (Rost, 1991). School culture and its leadership provide two resources to enable this change to occur. First, culture provides the source for change. As the organization struggles with solving the internal and external problems, the response to these problems originates in the culture in which teachers, administrators and students work and learn. School constituents start with their own values, beliefs, and assumptions and then adapt these to address the concerns and demands appropriately. Change begins with individuals acting in a leadership function to help schools consider what is not working and what needs to change. "In any group situation, some members will be more active than others and will propose verbally or by examples how things should be. These acts of leadership can come from different members at different times, but they are always there in some form or another" (Schein, 1992, p. 93).

Second, culture provides the energy for change. The best example of this is the way in which schools with strong cultures can nevertheless adapt to changing environmental demands. The cohesive and shared nature of their values and beliefs enables them to withstand the anxiety of considering changes. But principal leadership is critical here. Even strong cultures, as we will see, can be rigid, and anxiety can prohibit group members from considering change. Principal leaders provide "enough psychological safety to get members of their organization to accept the need for change and begin the traumatic learning process that is typically involved" (Schein, 1992, p. 333).

ILLUSTRATION

Spring Creek High School, in an affluent suburban community outside a major Midwestern city, has a strong culture dominated by norms of high student achievement and traditions of high expectations for academic, athletic and artistic accomplishments. However, when a new principal arrived and began to examine Spring Creek's student achievement records, he discovered that students who scored in the lowest third were largely ignored. The emphasis of the curriculum and instruction had been on the highest achievers to the exclusion of others. When he mentioned this finding to the math department head, her only comment was, "Well, obviously we're doing our job since we have so many students getting into the best colleges."

Clearly this department head expressed an assumption about the role of the school. How widely and strongly shared this assumption might be became a major question for the principal.

THE DARK SIDE OF CULTURE

We have celebrated the positive side of culture in terms of the advantages of shared values, norms, and beliefs. But, as Sergiovanni (1995) maintains, cultures have a "dark side." He quotes Karl Weick, "Strong cultures are tenacious cultures. Because a tenacious culture can be a rigid culture, that is slow to detect changes and opportunities and slow to change once opportunities are sensed, strong cultures can be backward, conservative instruments of adaptation" (Weick, 1985, p. 385).

Sergiovanni (1995) suggests two possible results of the dark side of culture. First, cultures may create the inability to perceive clearly what is real in both the organization and the environment. " . . . the presence of a strong norm system in a school can collectively program the minds of people so that issues of reality come into question. If this is carried to the extreme, the school might come to see reality in one way but its environment in another" (p. 111). Second, strong cultures can result in group members becoming less rational in their actions. In both instances, principal leadership is critical in providing disconfirming evidence, i.e., information that contradicts the shared vision of school members regarding the school's effectiveness and the environment's assessment.

THE METHODS OF LEADERSHIP FOR CULTURE

LEADERSHIP FOR CREATING CULTURE

Schein (1992, p. 231) identifies two sets of mechanisms that founders and leaders use to embed culture. The first set, "primary embedding mechanisms," includes the following:

- What leaders pay attention to, measure, and control on a regular basis.
- How leaders react to critical incidents and organizational crises.
- Observed criteria by which leaders allocate scarce resources.
- Deliberate role modeling, teaching, and coaching.

- Observed criteria by which leaders allocate rewards and status.

- Observed criteria by which leaders recruit, select, promote, retire, and excommunicate organizational members.

Principals in new schools, such as charter schools or redesigned schools, create culture by the activities and behavior to which they attend. If principals notice student self esteem concerns and emphasize these by their attention, behavioral norms that encourage student morale are likely to become a central feature of the school's culture. Furthermore, if resources are distributed in ways that emphasize one subject or grade level over another, these actions and their underlying values become part of the culture. Notice these are not atypical types of administrative behavior; on the contrary, they are routine parts of the administrator's role.

ILLUSTRATION

Ross Poore, principal of Northridge High School, north of Salt Lake City, was appointed a year before the building was completed. He and others designed the school to have technology as an integral part of the instruction and curriculum. Ross then went about hiring the faculty and staff to fit that culture and distributed resources to enhance the programs using technology. The school plant was designed to meet the physical needs of technology.

He was able to create a culture through hiring the faculty and staff, designing the building and allocating the resources needed to satisfy that value system. His task was to select staff with competence in the technologies but also compatible views about its uses in curriculum and instruction. During this selection process, Ross searched for ideas and suggestions that would enhance the view of education he was attempting to create and build a culture to support it.

As the culture of new organizations begins to develop, a second set of mechanisms acts as culture reinforcers (Schein, 1992, p. 245):

+ Organizational design and structure
+ Organizational systems and procedures
+ Organizational rites and rituals
+ Design of physical space, facades, and buildings
+ Stories, legends, and myths about people and events
+ Formal statements of organizational philosophy, values, and creed.

In the creation of school culture, principals use artifacts to embed and transmit the values and beliefs, and also basic underlying assumptions. The physical layout of the school; the kinds of dress encouraged; the language used to describe school activities and purposes; the ceremonies, rites and rituals that become associated with the school; and the behavioral expectations of teachers and students create and reinforce values and beliefs about how things are done at this school.

LEADERSHIP FOR MAINTAINING CULTURE

Most principals' work does not involve creating or changing culture but maintaining it. The culture itself acts as a strong influence on leaders and followers. But we believe there are realistic and relevant actions that principals can take to maintain a viable culture—that enables the school to solve its internal and external problems and that binds school staff, students, and parents together in community. In this section we will discuss how principals as leaders maintain school culture in addressing the needs of the three audiences identified earlier.

INTERNAL VETERANS

The principal's primary leadership role in maintaining culture is to reinforce school culture with internal veterans who are as much or more responsible for the culture as the principal. Reinforcement occurs through three vehicles: structures, routine activities, and subcultures.

As noted in the last section, as the school's culture matures, secondary mechanisms take hold to embed the culture. Among these secondary mechanisms are organizational structures, e.g., communication, reward, and decision making systems. The principal's role involves reinforcing these systems and using them to remind teachers and students of their purpose.

The second way principals reinforce school culture with internal veterans is through routine activities. "Cultures are built through the everyday business of school life. It is the way business is handled that both forms and reflects the culture....Culture building occurs through the way people use educational, human, and technical skills in handling daily events or establishing regular practices." (Saphier and King, 1985, p. 72). Studies of effective leaders have found that routine activities are commonly used vehicles for effecting change. "We observed an attention to the physical and emotional elements of the school environment, school-community relations, the teaching staff, schoolwide student achievement, and individual student progress. Their (the most effective principals') most essential activities included forms of monitoring, information control and exchange, planning, direct interaction with students, hiring and staff development, and overseeing building maintenance" (Dwyer, 1984, p.37).

Finally, principals reinforce culture with internal veterans by integrating subcultures. As school cultures develop over time, it is not surprising to find subcultures within the larger school organization also developing. These subcultures may include teachers, students, and parents with different goals and priorities for the school. The principal's leadership role becomes finding means to integrate these subcultures in ways that neither drain their vitality nor ignore the larger school culture's needs. However, while performing this integration function, principals must be sensitive to the importance of diversity within community (Crow, 1994). Integrating subcultures does not mean doing away with them.

INTERNAL NEWCOMERS

The second audience to which principals as leaders must address their attention in maintaining school culture is the group of internal newcomers who arrive on the scene after the culture is established. This role frequently gets overlooked by the principal and abdicated to veteran teachers or too often ignored altogether. If school cultures are to remain vital and vibrant, newcomers must be consciously socialized to the norms and values of the culture.

In the vignette, Richard Gonzales had a problem with three new teachers in his building. Perhaps, Richard's problem with these teachers was the lack of socialization into the school culture. Principals and veteran faculty often forget the importance of socialization with new teachers, leaving them the task of finding their own best way to integrate into the system.

Principals can accomplish the task of socializing newcomers through the artifacts that support the values and beliefs of the culture: celebrations, rituals, stories, and the emphasized language and behavior. The following table provides common school examples of these artifacts.

ARTIFACTS	SCHOOL EXAMPLES
celebrations	commencement and promotion exercises, award assemblies, proms, and other dances, Homecoming, retirement dinners
rituals	recess, reading as the first activity of the day, parent-teacher conferences, Halloween parades, pep rallies, spelling bees, faculty meetings, teacher preparation periods
stories	arts, sports, and academic traditions, founding fathers' historical traditions, famous alumnae, epics of renowned students or faculty
language	jokes, jargon of testing and special education placement, school mottoes, slogans, and songs, shields or crests, newsletters

Even in the midst of helping new teachers learn to survive, principals can socialize newcomers by what the principal attends to, how they deal with crises in the classroom, what kinds of behavior they reward, and how they respond to failures. Peters and Waterman (1982) argue that the leader's response to failure is as important as their response to success in building an innovative culture. If new teachers see attempts at innovation punished if they are unsuccessful, these new teachers are less likely to try them.

EXTERNAL CONSTITUENTS

In maintaining school culture, principals as leaders must communicate with external constituents. But instead of thinking of communication as a one way process where the principal expresses the values and beliefs of the school to the community, we see communication as a two-way street: In the vignette, Richard attempted to go to neighborhood meetings to discuss the new year round schedule. This was particularly difficult for him for two reasons. First, he had to carry a message that was not going to be well received (they do kill messengers). Second, he was not committed to the change himself. Richard, therefore, had to deal with both an internal conflict and an external conflict.

Besides getting resources from the external environment, communicating values and beliefs are critical in controlling external demands. This can be accomplished by enlarging the sphere of participants in the celebrations and rituals that are central to the school's culture. It also can be accomplished by making sure that the language used to express school values and beliefs is decipherable by community groups.

But there is a second direction to communication that involves listening to, being sensitive to, and addressing the concerns of external constituents. School cultures cannot remain vibrant, if they only emphasize the values and beliefs of staff members and ignore the concerns of the community. Due to this, principals must be actively involved in their communities, being sensitive to the ways communities are changing and to the views that external constituents have about what and how well schools are doing.

ILLUSTRATION

A hazing incident occurred among high school students in a small rural town. One high school boy was particularly offended by the incident and attempted to protest to the principal. Unable to gain any audience with the principal, the boy and his parents wrote a letter to the editor of a local newspaper. The news media became interested in the story and sought an interview with the school administrator. The principal turned down the opportunity for an interview and the media published the story without hearing both sides of the issue.

The school was unfairly tainted because the principal failed to communicate all the facts of the case. Many observers believe that if the principal had responded in a timely and sensitive manner to the student, parents, and the media, he could have saved the school from embarrassment.

Principals must balance the school's need for integration with the external community's need for the school to address its concerns. Too often the artifacts on which the values and beliefs of school culture are based are available only to insiders who know the "code." But such practices ignore the need to communicate with external constituents. Principals need to develop and reinforce rituals, celebrations, and stories that emphasize the school's cultural connection with the environment and that make sense to external as well as internal groups.

LEADERSHIP AND CHANGING CULTURE

We begin discussion in this section with an identification of situations when culture should change, and continue to an examination of specific actions that principals can take in helping to change the school culture.

WHEN IS CULTURAL CHANGE NEEDED?

Adapted from Deal and Kennedy (1982), the following are five situations when leaders should consider influencing the school to reshape its culture:

 ♦ When the environment is undergoing fundamental
    change.

 ♦ When education is highly competitive and the en-
    vironment changes quickly.

 ♦ When the school is mediocre or worse.

 ♦ When the school is truly at the threshold of
    becoming large.

 ♦ When the school is growing rapidly.

Many of these five situations can and often do overlap. For
example, in our vignette, Richard's school, Meadowlark
Elementary, is going through what many suburban schools do
in a period of rapid growth. The growth itself affects the
environment. Likewise, Carolyn's school, Central High, has
already gone through considerable change of demographics that
has affected its environment. Both schools are in need of a cultural
change.

ILLUSTRATION

Northwest Middle School, in Salt Lake City, is a school
where the demographics have shifted over the past fifteen
to twenty years. The school was once within a very middle
class, blue collar neighborhood. As the job market changed,
the school's demographics changed also. As the community
was going through this shift, it took a very strong and visionary principal to start a cultural change within the school.
Now, ten years later, the school is recognized as one of the
best in the state although its community is still economically
depressed.

Two key points about the school's cultural change in
this illustration are worth noting. One is that the change
is still in process even ten years after it began. Change does
not occur over night. Two, the principal who started the
change has left but the school continues to follow the same
collective vision.

Most school principals will attest to the fact that the environment of schools is undergoing phenomenal change (Odden,

1995). The changing demographics and diversity of student populations have created unforeseen challenges and opportunities for schools. The blurring speed of the knowledge explosion and the advent of technology have troubling consequences for school instruction and curriculum devised and based on earlier cultural foundations.

Current trends toward privatization including charter schools and schools of choice make education a competitive industry rarely seen since the arrival of the common school movement. It is not a certainty that public schools will continue to exist in the way they have in the past.

Since 1983, various commissions have catalogued the "mediocre" outcomes of schools. Although other writers (most recently, Berliner and Biddle, 1995) have questioned the accuracy of these assessments, the general perception of the public is that schools are not doing a good job of educating children for the future. In the 1995 Phi Delta Kappa/Gallup Poll (Elam and Rose, 1995), respondents expressed approval with the schools that their eldest child attended. In fact, 65 percent gave these schools an A or B. However, when asked to rate schools in the nation as a whole, only 20 percent gave them an A or B and 50 percent gave them a C.

Since the arrival of the comprehensive high school, educational organizations have been getting larger. Although reforms have recommended smaller, more communal schools, the trend is consistently toward larger schools.

All these factors illustrate the need to challenge cultural assumptions and determine whether these assumptions are successful in solving the environmental and internal problems of school organizations. Leaders and followers in individual schools may find that their cultural assumptions are appropriate for the community in which they live. However, the influence—some would say "intrusion"—of global change may make this assessment short-lived.

WHAT CAN LEADERS DO TO EFFECT CULTURAL CHANGE?

Once it is determined that school culture must change, principals can take several actions with followers and other leaders to change the culture. We will identify and discuss six types of action:

+ Start with yourself.

+ Exhibit emotional strength and sensitivity.

+ Diagnose the school's internal and external environment.

+ Involve others.

+ Select and socialize group members.

+ Use subcultures.

First, principals as leaders need to start with themselves. They must be sensitive to their own assumptions, values, and beliefs. "If they cannot learn new assumptions themselves, they will not be able to perceive what is possible in their organization" (Schein, 1992, p. 380). Leadership demands the ability to reflect on one's own practice as well as the practice of others (Schon, 1983; Hart and Bredeson, 1996). In the vignette, Richard and Carolyn are reflecting on their own assumptions about leadership, followership, and the role of the principal as a leader.

Second, principals as leaders need to exhibit the emotional strength and sensitivity to manage their own and others' anxieties in the face of change. Leaders must be sensitive to the anxiety created by change and respect the role that the past plays. Deal and Peterson (1990) label this function of the cultural leader as "healer." "The principal as healer recognizes the pain of transition and arranges events that make the transition a collective experience. Drawing people together to mourn loss and to renew hope is a significant part of the principal's culture-shaping role" (p. 30). In the vignette, Richard wants to help his teachers learn to take charge and develop leadership skills. Undoubtedly, in order to do this, he will need to help them work through their anxieties about responsibility.

Closely related to this idea is the role that mentors play with leaders. Although mentors in education have been mostly excluded except for short stints in the student teaching experience, the importance of mentors for school leaders has been clearly established (Daresh and Playko, 1992). As in the vignette with

Richard and Carolyn, a mentor can sometimes be simply a sounding board for a principal, someone who will listen and respond in conversation. Principals can become quite isolated from their colleagues. It often becomes necessary for principals to create their own mentors, much as Richard and Carolyn have done. Though this example was created by chance, a more deliberate approach should be taken by principals.

Third, the principal as leader must diagnose the school's situation to decide if the assumptions that form the basis of the culture work for the external demands and internal response necessary. This diagnostic ability also permits the leader to provide, if necessary, the disconfirming evidence that followers need to see before they agree that change is necessary.

Deal and Peterson (1990) suggest that the principal must be aware of past, present, and future in understanding the school's culture. They recommend several questions that will give the principal a way to understand school culture (pp. 17-19):

- How long has the school existed?
- Why was it built, and who were the first inhabitants?
- Who had a major influence on the school's direction?
- What critical incidents occurred in the past, and how were they resolved, if at all?
- What were the preceding principals, teachers, and students like?
- What does the school's architecture convey? How is space arranged and used?
- What subcultures exist inside and outside the school?
- Who are the recognized (and unrecognized) heroes and villains of the school?
- What do people say (and think) when asked what the school stands for? What would they miss if they left?
- What events are assigned special importance?

♦ How is conflict typically defined? How is it
  handled?

♦ What are the key ceremonies and stories of the
  school?

♦ What do people wish for? Are there patterns to
  their individual dreams?

The fourth thing principals as leaders can do to change school culture is to involve others in understanding the social realities of the environment and in diagnosing the current culture of the school. Only then will the influence relationship of leadership be viable for the health of the school culture. In the vignette, Carolyn seeks the cooperation of a teacher who has expertise in technology. But when she discovers that they disagree on where computers should be located, she drops the conversation. In so doing, she loses the perspective of a potentially critical individual in understanding and diagnosing the school culture.

Fifth, cultural change involves selecting teachers who hold the kinds of values that undergird the new cultural assumptions of the school. This sends a message of the kinds of values and beliefs that the leader is influencing followers to move toward. But socialization is also a critical tool to use in changing cultural assumptions of veterans (Crow, 1993; Ott, 1989). Socialization is especially powerful for veterans when "anxiety level is high, particularly when they are in a state of transition—crossing or preparing to cross organizational boundaries in order to enter new working groups and/or roles." (Ott, 1989, p. 90). In the vignette, the field trip incident undoubtedly raised the teachers' anxiety level due to the accident, and therefore provides a good opportunity for Richard to begin socializing his teachers to take on leadership roles.

Sixth, principals as leaders can use subcultures to change the school's assumptions, values, beliefs, and behavior. Subcultures can enhance the psychological safety needed to allow teachers, students, and parents to deal with the anxiety of change. They also remind organizational members of those aspects of the school's culture that are worth saving—the effective assumptions. Subcultures can provide the disconfirming information and the alternative assumptions that may need to be brought to light for the school to consider change. Rather than ignoring or attempting to get everyone to conform to the same set of assumptions, principals as leaders are wise to take advantage of the school's subcultures. Both Richard and Carolyn could identify groups of teachers in their schools that may be critical of the status quo. These groups may help the two principals work to change cultural assumptions in the school.

Akin to the use of subcultures is the use of the loyal opposition. "The task of the (loyal opposition) is to bring out the best in us. We need to be grateful for those who oppose us in a high-trust way, for they bring the picture of reality and practicality to our plans" (Block, 1987, p. 136). Again, rather than trying to get rid of opposition, leadership for changing culture should celebrate and use diversity, especially the diversity that challenges our assumptions.

In this chapter we have used the framework developed in Chapter 2 to understand leadership for creating, maintaining and changing school culture. Culture development is a major function of leadership in schools and, with the rapidly changing context in which contemporary schools find themselves, it has become a critical reason for realistic and relevant principal leadership.

REFLECTIVE VIGNETTE

The airplane food barely satisfied Richard's appetite. The food was tasty, but just not enough. Carolyn had talked during the entire meal and had hardly eaten anything. What she had said intrigued Richard. He could see that being a high school principal brought different challenges than being in the elementary school. He also recognized something he had never considered before. His elementary school was largely a neighborhood school. Most everyone came from the community. He never had any concern that parents would not be involved with the school. In fact, at times, he wished the parents were not quite as involved as they were. He related the incident with the petition against the three teachers as an example.

"So, Carolyn," asked Richard, "why does the district bus kids from all over to come to your school? Why not just allow the neighborhood kids to come?"

"The idea is," Carolyn began, "to allow for diversity. You see, we have different socioeconomic groups and different racial and cultural groups from various neighborhoods. We have the philosophy that we have a better school when as many of these groups can mix as possible. It does bring diversity but it also brings some problems, such as gang related incidents. We also lack parental involvement with the parents from outlying areas. They just cannot get into the school very often when they have so far to travel. Maybe on parent nights we should have school buses run for parents like they do for kids," Carolyn added amusingly.

Richard contemplated the idea of diversity for a moment and then responded. "I see the advantage for diversity but I also see the advantage of neighborhood schools. I believe that is why the school board in our district wanted my school to go year round rather than to bus the kids to outlying schools."

Richard continued, "In our school we have basically the same groups. When a new kid arrives in the community, he or she sometimes finds it hard to fit in at first. Kids, and their parents, can be cruel at times. If you are part of the 'in group' everything is just fine. But most new kids don't have the foggiest idea of what the 'in group' involves and so they often aren't well accepted. We have had families move away just to remove their kids from the situation. But, then again, we don't have much gang activity either."

Carolyn sipped at her coffee as she thought about Richard's school. She could almost see the elementary school in her mind. All of the bulletin boards would have colored displays, the floors would be shiny from last night's waxing, the halls would always be orderly, and when kids were in the halls they would be lined up, the young and enthusiastic teachers would be fitting the kids with gloves and coats. A flash of her own high school entered her mind. She could not remember the last time they waxed the halls, the tile was so old it was yellowed. The students wore every style, fashion, fad and trend in clothes. Some were totally unacceptable and the students had to be sent home, a punishment not wholly disliked or unplanned. In the mornings, the halls would be a scene similar to a department store having a clearance sale, with kids and teachers madly running to make it on time. The teachers, especially the middle-aged males, had long since lost their spunk. They were waiting it out, knowing that they would get paid the same if they were good or not. The female teachers were often referred to as the "old guard." The old guard protected the traditions of the school and held onto memories of when it was considered the best in the city. Carolyn also felt they desired the return of their former male principal, and not this high flying female they had now.

"You know," Richard thought aloud, "we both have different cultures and with that a different set of problems. Changing the cultures in both schools will be as difficult. I just hope I have enough fire in my belly to stand up to the task."

"I hope I have enough patience!" Carolyn responded.

SELF-REFLECTION ACTIVITIES

♦ Refer to the last two sentences in the vignette. What does Richard mean when he says he hopes he has enough fire in his belly to stand up to the task of change? What does Carolyn mean in her last statement?

♦ Consider yourself the principal of Carolyn's school with a faculty that was content to let you administer as you wished. What are the advantages and disadvantages of persuading the faculty to become more involved in maintaining and changing the school culture?

PEER-REFLECTION ACTIVITIES

+ Reflect on the two schools in the vignette. Is there a point at which an elementary school or a secondary school can become too large? What effect does size have on the culture of your school?

+ Discuss with a peer the ways the technology explosion can affect school culture.

+ Together determine times when loyal opposition has been good and when it has been harmful to your school's growth.

+ Together reflect on this statement: "Cultures do not develop full blown, nor are they maintained without effort nor changed without anxiety."

COURSE ACTIVITIES

+ Compare and contrast the two cultures described in both schools in the vignette? Locate evidence to support your answer. How does each principal create and maintain the culture?

+ Debate this proposition: Followers are more important than leaders in maintaining culture.

+ Refer to the table on page 65. Expand the examples of artifacts such as celebrations, rituals, stories, and language, based on your experience.

+ Deal and Peterson (1990) suggest that the principal must be aware of past, present, and future in understanding the school's culture. Select a school and research the thirteen questions on pages 71–72. Report the findings to the entire class.

+ What advantages and disadvantages are there for neighborhood schools in establishing culture? How does busing affect culture?

4

INFLUENCING A COLLECTIVE VISION

Perhaps the most overused and underappreciated word in the principal-leadership vocabulary is *vision*. During the effective schools movement, this term became a rallying cry for ensuring a relevant role for school administrators. Yet it was not well understood nor well conceptualized and its use emphasized an unrealistic view of the principal's role in the construction of vision. Used in the heroic imagery of principals as sole leaders, *vision* came to mean something principals alone possess. Principals were encouraged to develop a strategic vision and then "sell it" to teachers, parents, and students. However, we will argue in this chapter that vision can and should involve a collective process. This collective vision need not diminish the realistic and relevant role of the principal in developing and communicating school vision.

THE NATURE OF LEADERSHIP FOR VISION

In understanding the nature of leadership for constructing and communicating a school vision, it is important to understand what vision is and what leaders and followers do to influence each other in constructing a collective vision.

WHAT IS VISION?

We distinguish two types of vision: the principal's personal vision and the organization's collective vision. While the two may be similar, even identical, they should be distinguished.

PERSONAL VISION

The principal as leader should have a vision of the purpose of schooling, the goal of teaching and learning, and how these can be accomplished in the lives of students. This personal vision includes values, goals, direction, and purpose. It focuses and energizes the principal's actions and forms the basis for what the principal seeks to influence followers to become and to do.

This personal vision focuses the principal's work, providing the basis for decisions and actions. Probably the most useful finding of the effective schools literature regarding principal leadership is that the rationale or vision that guides the routine activities of administrators differentiates effective from ineffective principals (Dwyer, 1984). Effective principals have a personal vision that concentrates their attention and provides the passion for one activity over another.

"The leader's vision is what motivates him or her to be a genuine player in the drama and is a call to greatness as well. The leader's vision is also what enables him or her to articulate the major themes of the drama in the role of director. The vision enables the leader/director to see the unity within the various scenes and subplots of the drama, and to call the various actors to express, in their own parts, those overarching themes" (Starratt, 1993, p. 145). This perspective involves the leader's own purpose and understanding of the organization's mission and provides the fervor that motivates and ennobles the principal's work.

Besides focusing and energizing the principal's own work, the personal vision also provides the basis for the principal's leadership role in influencing the collective vision. The preliminary vision may prompt the conversations with school constituents about a shared view of the school's direction and purpose.

COLLECTIVE VISION

School organizations need a shared vision. This is the collective picture of what leaders and followers together construct regarding the values, beliefs, and assumptions of the school and what it should look like in the future. Seeley (1992) identifies two parts of this collective or organizational vision. Using Cuban's (1988) first and second order changes, Seeley identifies programmatic vision and systemic vision.

The programmatic vision refers to specific kinds of programs or teaching/learning content that direct the school staff's efforts. An example of a programmatic vision is a particular kind of reading program that focuses teaching and learning.

Systemic vision, comparable to Cuban's second-order change, focuses on broader organizational directions. Restructuring or reconceptualizing the organization's roles, rules, relationships, and responsibilities are parts of the school's systemic vision. Leaders and followers visualize how new sets of expectations, relationships, and structures fit together into a coherent whole. An example of a systemic vision is restructuring how decisions regarding instructional program and materials are made.

Besides programmatic or systemic elements, collective visions serve present and future functions. Visions provide the energy, inspiration, and motivation for administrators, teachers, students, parents and community members to work toward a common purpose. If a vision exists to provide direction, our current actions have more meaning. Further, collective visions serve a future function. The vision serves as "a signpost pointing the way for all who need to understand what the organization is and where it intends to go" (Nanus, 1992, p. 9). In this way, the school's work moves beyond simply day to day activities, toward a sense of the future.

These two types of vision—personal and collective—come together as the leader attempts to influence followers to construct a collective vision. "…[T]he leader must encourage the members to fashion a collective vision of where they should be going. This means spending a large portion every day engaging the minds and hearts of his or her constituents in examining how they are reproducing the status quo every day and how they might alter it in small ways to make the drama of their institution work better for the people it serves and who serve it. As they take up that task, they are improving, in some small way, the larger social drama of history" (Starratt, 1993, p. 149).

INFLUENCING THE COLLECTIVE VISION

Leaders and followers influence collective vision as to both process and content. The principal as leader must attend to each of these in influencing the school's vision.

THE PROCESS OF VISION

Typically we talk only about the content of vision—the direction or purpose to which the school is headed. Yet vision is also a process by which individuals fashion a direction for the organization. It "involves sharing ideas, clarifying and understanding the various points of view reflected in the community as well as the beliefs and assumptions underneath those points of view, negotiating differences and building a consensus" (Starratt, 1996, p. 50).

Influencing vision entails the use of the power resources we identified in Chapter 2, e.g., expertise, rewards, loyalty, and charisma. Leaders and followers use these resources in exchanging ideas, negotiating purpose, and building consensus. The influence process is not a necessary evil. Instead, it is a positive part of fashioning a collective vision to which both leaders and followers can commit.

The result of this influence process is a "bonding" (Sergiovanni, 1995) between leaders and followers. This bonding provides the commitment to the vision. If no bonding has occurred, that is, no compact or agreement made on the direction the organization should take, then the result is a vision that neither leaders nor followers will commit to and pursue into the future. An example of this is the number of school strategic plans where teachers and principals go through the motion of strategic planning without committing to implementation.

THE CONTENT OF VISION

The influence process focuses on a conception of what the future should look like for this school. Principals as leaders help others construct a "realistic, credible, attractive future" picture for their school (Nanus, 1992, p. 8). They "may not possess the total content of the vision—no one does—but they should be willing to lay out a first attempt at articulating the content of a vision" (Starratt, 1996, p.50).

Principals can perform a relevant leadership role by providing this realistic, credible, and attractive picture. They accomplish this by being sensitive to the complexity of the external environment (Weick, 1978)—its threats and opportunities—and the potential of the internal environment. Visions are not created "out of nothing." They include elements of the organization's culture and practice already prized by leaders and followers. Westley and Mintzberg (1988) compare Rene Levesque, the advocate for an autonomous state of Quebec, and Lee Iacocca, former chairman of Chrysler, about how they developed vision. In Levesque's case, he defined a specific vision early in the process that was eaten away by forming coalitions and building support. In contrast, Iacocca's process was analogous to a sort of "garbage collector with artistic genius." He looked for useful bits of organizational components and values and built them into an essential content. Then as he formed coalitions and built support, the process of using what was already there increased the likelihood that followers would commit to the vision.

The content of the vision, Sergiovanni (1995) argues, "should not be construed as a strategic plan that functions like a road map charting the turns needed to reach a specific reality that the leader has in mind. It should, instead, be viewed more as a compass that points the direction to be taken, that inspires enthusiasm, and that allows people to buy into and take part in the shaping of the way that will constitute the school's mission" (pp. 163–164).

THE PARTICIPANTS OF LEADERSHIP FOR VISION

The principal is traditionally described as "the vision holder, the keeper of the dream, or the person who has a vision of the organization's purpose" (Mundez-Morse, 1995, p. 3). This view is unrealistic given the complexity of environmental changes and the enormity of the task. Nevertheless, the principal has a relevant and realistic leadership role to play in the development of a collective vision.

The principal's leadership role must also recognize that others besides the principal play leadership roles in this process. These other individuals may be both leaders and followers. In fact, at times the principal may play a follower role and a leader role.

LEADER'S ROLE IN VISION

Nanus (1992) suggests four roles that the visionary leader plays based on two dimensions: time and environmental sphere. The first role is *direction-setter*. This role focuses on the future and the external environment. The visionary leader as direction-setter "selects and articulates the target in the future external environment toward which the organization should direct its energies" (p. 12). The second role is *change agent*. This role emphasizes the future as well but focuses on the internal environment. Here the visionary leader is "responsible for catalyzing changes in the internal environment...to make the vision achievable in the future" (p. 13). The third role is *spokesperson*, which directs attention to the present and external environment. The visionary leader "as a skilled speaker, a concerned listener, and the very embodiment of the organization's vision—is the chief advocate and negotiator for the organization and its vision with outside constituencies" (p. 14). Finally, the visionary leader is a *coach*. This is a present function within the internal environment. "The leader is a team builder who empowers individuals in the organization and passionately 'lives the vision,' thereby serving as a mentor and example for those whose efforts are necessary to make the vision become reality" (Nanus, 1992, p. 14).

ILLUSTRATION

In 1988, Mary Bancroft developed a writing curriculum using computers in her fifth grade classroom at Polk Elementary. Over time, the excitement of the students for writing and their progress in skill development helped to create interest throughout the school for such a writing program. Mary's efforts served to set direction and eventually

---

create change for the writing program for the entire school as teachers sought her out for observation and inservice. She now serves as a state wide resource person coaching teachers in other schools, interested in developing a writing program, and in so doing acts as a spokesperson for her school.

These four roles are useful in understanding the principal's responsibility beyond a sole authorship function. In fact, the actual vision construction occurs only in combination with followers. The leader may identify those issues of the external environment that prompt the need for constructing a vision along some line or for "revisioning," but it is in combination with followers that the actual vision construction occurs.

As noted in the previous section, it is not atypical for the leader's personal vision to serve as a preliminary conception from which the collective vision is constructed. Yet this personal vision must not become the final word. Preliminary visions may serve as guides to immediate action and places to begin conversations about collective visions, but they should not serve as sole directions for the future.

Beyond constructing and communicating vision, leaders also critique vision, i.e., they lead followers to evaluate the effectiveness and application of a vision for new or changed conditions. This critiquing role also suggests a "teaching" function to the principal's visionary role. "Leaders can also shape and alter and elevate the motives and values and goals of followers through the vital teaching role of leadership. This is transforming leadership. The premise of this leadership is that, whatever the separate interests persons might hold, they are presently and potentially united in the pursuit of 'higher' goals, the realization of which is tested by the achievement of significant change that represents the collective or pooled interests of leaders and followers" (Burns, 1978, pp. 425–426).

FOLLOWERS' ROLE IN VISION

Followers also have a leadership role to play in vision. "Because our emphasis is on collective purpose and change, we stress the factors that unite leaders and followers as well as those that differentiate them. This distinction may be elusive to an observer who sees leaders leading followers but does not understand that leaders may modify their leadership in recognition of followers' preferences, or in order to anticipate followers' responses, or in order to harmonize the actions of both leader and follower with their common motives, values, and goals. Leaders and followers are engaged in a common enterprise, they are dependent on each other, their fortunes rise and fall together, they share the results of planned change together" (Burns, 1978, p. 426).

Followers play at least three roles in visionary leadership: source of vision, sustainer of vision, and critic of vision. As a source of vision, followers may actually provide the image or picture of the future. "Often some of the best ideas for new directions float up from the depths of the organization, but only if they are sought and welcomed when they arrive" (Nanus, 1992, p. 38). Because students and teachers are engaged in the core activity of the school, they may be in a better position to create new visions of teaching and learning that provide direction to the school. Their pictures of what the school can be should be taken seriously and encouraged.

Followers are also sustainers of vision. Without them visions would wither. They are the ones who must be committed to the achievement of the vision. Serious attempts to attain these visions are ultimately in the hands and hearts of followers. Their belief that a particular vision will work for this school at this time, to engage it and direct it, is critical to the vision process.

Finally, followers are critics of visions. Leaders should listen carefully and sensitively to what followers are saying about the saliency of visions. Followers provide leaders those indications of whether visions are working or whether "revisioning" is needed. In the vignette segment at the end of this chapter, an incident is described by Richard in which he attempted to implement a whole language program in his elementary school. The teachers acted as critics to remind Richard of the disruption this would cause if it were implemented as quickly as Richard wanted.

These three functions are an integral part of school life. Sub-cultures form, opinion leaders arise to champion them, and inter-actions occur to shape and refine them. Within sets of dynamic relationships, attitudes and beliefs are formed, work habits reinforced, standards are set, and issues are discussed. Followers and informal groupings of them shape the school's vision of what it is and can become. School principals, if they are to lead, need to be keen observers of the dynamics that shape the vision of the school either to enhance or impede its improvement.

PRINCIPALS AS LEADERS OF LEADERS FOR VISION

Beyond these previously identified leader and follower roles, principals serve a major function of leading others to be visionary leaders. Principals encourage teachers, students, and parents to be direction-setters, change agents, spokespersons, and coaches (Nanus, 1992). These roles are too immense and too critical to be performed by one person in the school. Yet the principal more than any other individual must take the responsibility of encouraging and supporting the development of others to be leaders of vision.

A major way principals lead other visionary leaders is to acknowledge the powerful personal visions that teachers bring to the school. Typically, these visions are overlooked. "All of us who entered teaching brought with us a conception of a desirable school. Each of us had a personal vision and was prepared to work, even fight, for it. Over time, our personal vision became blurred by the visions, demands, and requirements of others. Many teachers' personal views are now all but obliterated by external prescriptions" (Barth, 1986, p. 478).

Principals lead leaders by acknowledging the unique content of teachers' visions. Teachers can bring a sensitivity to classroom and student needs that is often ignored in the larger vision of the school. At times administrative visions of restructuring ignore the core activity of schools. If teachers' visions are ignored or discounted, the school's direction for teaching and learning will suffer. Principals have the indispensable role of encouraging the expression of teachers' personal visions. No one else can serve this function as effectively and forcefully as principals.

THE LOCATION OF LEADERSHIP FOR VISION

In this section, we elaborate on the principal's visionary leadership role in the external and internal spheres.

THE EXTERNAL SPHERE OF LEADERSHIP FOR VISION

Developing a picture of what the school organization should look like in the future begins with an understanding of the external environment. Here the demands and changes intrude on the school in ways that require an assessment of the vision's effectiveness that may result in the need for a new vision. The external environment for schools is shifting toward rapidly changing technologies and more heterogeneous student populations (Odden, 1995). This context tests how adequate current visions are. In response to this, principals have two critical roles to play in the external sphere: attention to these changes and communication of school visions.

First, principals as leaders need to be aware of what changes are occurring in the external environment that may impinge on schools. Listening sensitively and critically to parents and community groups, principals can attend to the ways schools are or are not meeting students' needs as they prepare to live in a world different from their parents. Listening sensitively to external voices, some quiet and others loud, permits principals to hear the changes that are being sought and to begin to develop appropriate responses.

Principals also play a leadership role in the external sphere by communicating the school's collective vision to external constituents. For principals in schools of choice, this role has become increasingly critical (Crow, 1992). These principals are required to express the school's vision so that parents can make choices regarding which school direction most adequately meets their children's needs. However, the time has arrived when all principals need to be able to communicate clearly the school's collective vision. The old public school monopoly is less frequently seen and all principals are facing entrepreneurial roles—marketing the school's vision to community members and parents.

Increasingly principals are expected to be "consumer responsive." Although parents favor choice, they have not generally selected choice as a viable option for their children. However, parents are more demanding as to the type of education their child is receiving within the school. This perhaps could be termed "choice within schools." The authors have been working with several schools in which parents and students now have choice of the teachers whom they will take. Although this has occurred on a minimal level with some parents for decades, these schools have actually advertised the fact that parents do have a choice of teachers. In one high school as an example, a student selects the algebra class and the teacher for the class when he or she registers. Surprisingly, this high school reports that few significant problems have occurred with the opening of this traditionally and sometimes sacred school rite. This practice has added another dimension to communicating the school's vision and working within the internal sphere, as will be discussed in the next section.

THE INTERNAL SPHERE OF LEADERSHIP FOR VISION

Principals also have leadership roles to play in the school's internal sphere. The first role involves influencing school constituents to develop responses to the external demands while maintaining internal integration. At times this means providing disconfirming information, which demonstrates the ineffective ways the school is meeting the needs of students and families, and the psychological safety to risk changing these ways. At other times, this role means communicating the school's real achievements to cynical external constituents.

The second leadership role that principals play in the internal sphere is the "coach" role (Nanus, 1992). In this role, principals cheer the school on toward vision achievement. This coaching and cheering function occurs by what the principal pays attention to, rewards, and celebrates. Even school staff whose vision effectively addresses a changing environment need to be encouraged and inspired.

In the internal sphere of leadership, principals also motivate the faculty toward higher standards of teaching. This becomes critical when parents and students have the opportunity to select the school and the teacher. Teachers truly have to advertise their "wares." Principals are constantly working within this sphere, stimulating the further professional growth of teaching and learning.

Principals provide a visionary leadership role in both external and internal spheres. To ignore one in favor of the other is to abdicate leadership responsibility. Although others may play these roles, principals have the critical responsibility to ensure that these roles are effectively enacted and to encourage and support the leadership role of others in performing these responsibilities.

THE PURPOSE OF LEADERSHIP FOR VISION

We could argue that principals have always played a central leadership role in articulating and reminding school staff of their purpose and direction. Nevertheless, contemporary schools in a changing society need visionary leadership from the principal in more intensive ways and for different reasons. With the changing demographics of students, the exploding technologies, and democratization trends (Odden, 1995), principals face a more difficult job in keeping the purpose of schooling clearly in the minds and hearts of school constituents, both inside and outside school. Moreover, the chances that the school's vision will need to be reexamined and possibly revised are much greater in a dynamic environment than in the static, homogeneous environment of the past.

In this type of changing environment, examining visions is an ongoing process. Reorganization is another contemporary issue that requires vision to be an ongoing concern for leaders and followers (Vaill, 1984). It is an unusual school that has been ignored in the restructuring or reorganization frenzy of contemporary educational reform. Nevertheless, frequently school leaders enact restructuring agendas without a simultaneous consideration of whether the school's vision fits with these reforms. "The impact of these changes on role relationships, chains of command, felt sense of accountability, etc., is not as thoroughly discussed as it should be, particularly the impact of all this flux on purpose" (Vaill, 1984, p. 90). Reforms that affect the internal integration of schools without considering how these changes modify the school's vision not only risk failure of the reforms but, much worse, leave the school in disarray.

These external and internal environmental changes suggest three major purposes of the principal's visionary leadership: direction, means, and energy. The principal provides direction to the vision process and content. This is not to suggest that followers or other leaders have no role in constructing the vision but rather that the principal as leader has a primary responsibility for providing direction to the process, i.e., to keep school constituents' "eyes on the prize." That direction needs to emphasize the central importance of human growth in and for community (Crow and Slater, 1996).

The second purpose of the principal's visionary leadership is to provide the means for constructing and examining vision. The shared vision necessary to move a school toward some purpose must involve a collective process that includes leaders and followers. Sharing concerns, hopes, dreams and strategies is not only necessary for arriving at the "right" vision but ensuring that vision has a better chance of being achieved.

Third, the principal as visionary leader provides the energy for reexamining and constructing vision. This is the inspirational role necessary for school constituents to persist with a process that may be uncomfortable, even frightening. The principal's commitment and passion to the vision process is critical in finding a direction that improves students' educational experiences and teachers' work lives.

VISIONS THAT BLIND

Just as culture has a dark side, vision also has a dark side; it can blind the leader and the organization. Fullan (1992) suggests three ways leaders can be blinded by visions. First, "the leader who is committed to a particular innovation may pursue it in such a narrow and self-defeating way that teachers resist the idea" (p. 19). Stories abound of principals who become so enamored with their personal vision of an innovation in teaching or the organization of the school that they create confusion and resentment among staff. In these situations, no collective vision exists, only the principal's personal vision.

Second, visions can blind school staff when the leader "is successful in getting teachers to use the innovation but fails to achieve more basic changes that would enable them to consider alternatives and reflect on their practice" (p. 19). The dynamic nature of environments—both internal and external—requires an ongoing vision process rather than fixation on one innovation. Reflective practice is not a luxury but a necessity in contemporary schools.

Third, visions can blind school staff in the case of the "charismatic leader where so much depends on personal strength or pressure but innovation is short-lived" (p. 19). This is one reason we have tried in this book to present a realistic and relevant leadership role for principals. The old heroic imagery and charisma required of principals are not realistic for most principals nor is it particularly valuable for creating a collective vision.

One answer to the issue of blinding visions is to see the principal's leadership role as one of "enabler of solutions" rather than a problem solver (Fullan, 1992). This moves us back to the principal as "leader of leaders" role—supporting, teaching, and encouraging others to solve problems and create visions. This relevant role conception of the principal encourages the consideration of alternative visions and the development of a shared direction.

METHODS OF LEADERSHIP FOR VISION

We will identify and discuss four major actions that principals can take to provide visionary leadership (Mundez-Morse, 1995; Nanus, 1992).

+ Understand the school and its environment
+ Involve critical individuals
+ Explore possible future pictures
+ Develop/communicate vision

UNDERSTAND THE SCHOOL AND ITS ENVIRONMENT

Before any collective vision can be developed, a clear understanding of the school organization and its environment must be available to both leaders and followers. The principal's responsibility is to provide that understanding or arrange for others to develop an understanding of the school's internal and external environments.

Nanus (1992, pp. 190–224) suggests conducting a vision audit, considering a vision scope, and understanding the vision context. The following lists present some of his questions pertinent to each of these activities.

THE VISION AUDIT

♦ What is the current stated mission or purpose of your organization?

♦ What does it take for your organization to succeed?

♦ What are the values and the organizational culture that govern behavior and decision making?

♦ If the organization continues on its current path, where will it be heading over the next decade? How good would such a direction be?

THE VISION SCOPE

♦ Who are the major stakeholders—both inside and outside your organization—and of these, which are the most important?

♦ What are the major interests and expectations of the five or six most important stakeholders regarding the future of your organization?

♦ What threats or opportunities emanate from these critical stakeholders?

♦ Considering yourself a stakeholder, what do you personally and passionately want to make happen in your organization?

THE VISION CONTEXT

♦   What major changes can be expected in the needs and wants served by your organization in the future?

♦   What major changes can be expected in the relevant economic environments in the future?

♦   What major changes can be expected in the relevant social environments in the future?

♦   What major changes can be expected in the relevant political environments in the future?

♦   What major changes can be expected in the relevant technological environments in the future?

♦   Which future developments would have the most impact on your choice of vision, and what are the probabilities of these high-priority developments actually occurring?

These questions focus attention on the future as well as the present. Too often visions are not future oriented directions but static present beliefs about what currently exists. Given the changing environments we have documented, an exploration of future possibilities is not simply an interesting mental exercise; it is a necessary process for arriving at a school vision.

Some principals may complain that there is no need to change visions and therefore no need to go through these exercises in understanding the internal, external, present, and future environments. Perhaps this is the case, yet perhaps not. Nanus (1992, pp. 19-20) identifies eight warning signs that suggest the need to revise the school's vision. His questions are adapted to school situations:

♦   Is there evidence of confusion about purpose?

♦   Do teachers complain about insufficient challenge or say they're not having fun anymore? Are they pessimistic about the future or cynical about the present?

♦   Is the school losing legitimacy, market position, or its reputation for innovation?

- Does the school seem out-of-tune with trends in the environment?

- Are there signs of a decline in pride within the school?

- Is there excessive risk avoidance, with people abiding by their narrow job descriptions, unwilling to accept ownership or responsibility for new projects or resisting change?

- Is there an absence of a shared sense of progress or momentum?

- Is there a hyperactive rumor mill, with people constantly trying to find out through the grapevine what is in store for them or the school?

Thus before a vision can be constructed, leaders and followers need a clear understanding of the school's internal, external, present, and future environments. The principal is in the best position to provide information and to engage leaders and followers in understanding and using this contextual information for building a collective vision.

Involve Critical Individuals in the Process

Besides understanding what key stakeholders, both inside and outside the school, perceive the school's vision to be, these individuals need to be included in the vision development process. These critical individuals must be included at this early stage of the process for the vision to be collective and achievable.

Three groups of individuals need to be included in conversations about vision: (1) parents, school board members, community leaders, and central office administrators; (2) teachers; and (3) students (Starratt, 1996). For the first group, the discussions need to focus on those community needs, expectations, and concerns that influence what the school teaches, what students learn, and what services the school provides. "In these conversations, however, the administrators are not simply taking soundings from the community; they are actively promoting their best ideas about the purposes of schooling. In other words, they are not simply assessing public opinion; they are also helping to shape public opinion" (Starratt, 1996, p.64).

Conversations with teachers should involve bringing the concerns and issues provided by the community to their attention as well as engaging them in discussions of how the nature of knowledge is changing. Teachers should also be engaged in assessments of the current learning situation and the implications of the environmental and knowledge issues for how teaching and learning should occur now and in the future.

Finally, students are critical for discussions of vision. They provide assessments of the school's learning environment and their involvement in learning. Students are vital to the vision process in part because they are not only the ultimate recipients of what the school provides but a primary partner in how the vision is shaped and achieved. In contrast to the traditional role of students simply as recipients of information provided by teachers, contemporary notions of learning emphasize that students and teachers co-construct learning (Brown, 1989; Sockett, 1987).

EXPLORE POSSIBLE VISIONS OF THE FUTURE

Principals need to lead other school leaders and followers to understand possible future developments in economic, social, political, and technological environments. One reason for this understanding is to provide information that can be used to project possible visions of where the school can and should be in the future.

Yet beyond these cognitive elements of understanding present, future, internal and external contexts lies another ingredient. Shekerjian (1990), who studied MacArthur Award winners, found that great ideas came from both instinct and judgment. "What intuition provides is an inkling, an itch, a yearning, a list of possibilities. What judgment provides is structure, assessment, form, and purpose" (p. 170). Frequently in education we pursue the rational side to the exclusion of the intuitive, imaginative side. Yet visions are both rational understandings of future developments and imaginative forays into what is creative and possible.

"Vision is composed of one part foresight, one part insight, plenty of imagination and judgment, and often, a healthy dose of chutzpah. It occurs to a well-informed open mind, a mind prepared by a lifetime of learning and experience, one sharply attuned to emerging trends and developments in the world outside of the organization. Creativity certainly plays an important part, but it is a creativity deeply rooted in the reality of the organization and its possibilities" (Nanus, 1992, p. 34).

DEVELOP AND COMMUNICATE THE VISION

Based on a solid understanding of the internal and external environments and the present and future situation and possibilities, and pursued by critical individuals engaged in judgment and imagination, a collective vision develops. Still, how do we choose the "right vision"? Perhaps the following questions are useful in evaluating a vision (Nanus, 1992):

♦ Is it appropriate for the organization and for the times?

♦ Does it set standards of excellence and reflect high ideals?

♦ Does it clarify purpose and direction?

♦ Does it inspire enthusiasm and encourage commitment?

♦ Is it well articulated and easily understood?

♦ Does it reflect the uniqueness of the organization, its distinctive competence, what it stands for, and what it is able to achieve?

♦ Is it ambitious?

Communicating the vision is also critical for achieving the vision. Written vision statements should be prepared for at least two reasons. First, being able to write down a vision statement makes commitment possible. Oral tradition is an important part of school culture, but visions should go beyond this to written statements for newcomers and veterans to use to assess the organization's attempts to move in the agreed direction. Second, being able to write down a vision is an indication of its clarity and sense. Visions must be understood to be achieved.

Besides writing a statement, visions are communicated by expression in action. The principal has a primary leadership role in expressing the school's vision. Sashkin (1988) suggests five ways that the principal expresses the vision: focusing attention on specific elements of the vision, communicating personally (e.g., active listening, giving feedback effectively, and being specific rather than general), displaying trustworthiness (i.e., say what you mean and mean what you say), displaying respect (i.e., toward one self and others), and taking risks.

When principals express the collective vision in their daily activities, they influence other leaders and followers to believe in and commit to this vision. Herein lies a major way principals can play a realistic and relevant role in leadership for vision.

REFLECTIVE VIGNETTE

"I'm sure I can convince my faculty about the need for this technology grant," Carolyn said trying to convince herself. "They are often reluctant at first, but they usually jump on board after I get things rolling."

Richard had to contemplate that for a while before he responded. He knew he would have a difficult time with that approach with his faculty. He told Carolyn about an experience he had when he first became a principal. It was about fifteen years ago when he had thought that the whole language reading approach would be a better method to adopt at his elementary school. He had just returned from a conference on whole language reading and he was enthusiastic about it and tried to convince the faculty that this was the latest and best way to teach both reading and writing. He was ready to replace the basal readers immediately with the new whole language approach. He was not prepared for what followed. Not one teacher in the elementary school agreed with or supported implementing the new approach that fast. He grinned about it as he told Carolyn how he had to manage a small mutiny among the teachers. "I had to reconsider the time schedule and allow the idea to grow from within the faculty. It took more time that way, but the results came out the same. Eventually we went to the whole language approach. So, I guess 'all's well that ends well.'"

Carolyn carefully considered what Richard was saying. She liked his easy, frank, and open personality. His years of experience had developed into considerable wisdom in working with people. She wanted to learn more. "Let me ask you a question," she queried. "How do you handle a situation in which you know something is best for the school, but your faculty hasn't grasped the vision of it yet?"

"Well, I've been in that situation a hundred times. I have come to realize that my vision is not what counts. It is the vision of the faculty that really matters. If I think something is important that we should be considering, I try to expose as many teachers to it as I can. If they think it is important, it will catch on. I then just have to facilitate it rather than direct it."

Carolyn's mind was racing. At first she thought that her school was so different from his that she could never do that. As she thought more about what Richard had said, it occurred to her that having computers in the school accomplishes little unless the teachers are willing and able to incorporate them into the curriculum and the instruction. She started her Toshiba laptop and opened the file with the grant. She was about to amend the proposal.

SELF-REFLECTION ACTIVITIES

◆ In the vignette Carolyn's approach to initiating change is more direct while Richard's is more subtle. What are the advantages and disadvantages of each approach? Are there situations that warrant each approach?

◆ Consider Richard's attempt to implement the whole language approach in his school. Have you experienced a situation in which the principal attempted to implement something only to find a faculty resistant? What was the eventual outcome?

♦ How would you describe your school's collective vision? How did it develop? Ask veterans in your school how they have seen the vision evolve over the years.

♦ Reflect on whether your school policies and practices manifest the vision of the school.

PEER-REFLECTIVE ACTIVITIES

♦ Consider Carolyn's technology grant proposal. What approach should she take to influence others to accept her personal vision as the school's collective vision?

♦ What approach can a principal pursue when his or her vision for the school is different from the vision of the teachers?

♦ With a peer, discuss how students are critical for the development of a collective vision. Identify ways you could involve students in developing a collective vision for your school.

COURSE ACTIVITIES

♦ Discuss Nanus' four roles of a visionary leader: direction setter, change agent, spokesperson, and coach. Apply these four roles to a particular principal(s).

♦ The movie *Lean on Me* is based on the career of Joe Clark, an inner city principal who used dramatic means to change the school's vision. View the movie and apply the principles discussed in this chapter to the dimensions of his practice.

♦ Oral tradition is important but written visions are essential. Review different school vision statements and interview those who were involved in developing the statements. Report on how the vision statements were developed.

5

LEADERSHIP FOR SCHOOL IMPROVEMENT: INFLUENCING AN ENVIRONMENT FOR CHANGE

In the late 1970s with the arrival of the school effectiveness literature, the image of the principal shifted from a "gatekeeper" role to that of "instructional leadership" in relation to school improvement (Fullan, 1992). However, as research de-emphasized the principal as essential to the success of particular change projects and identified organizational factors and roles that could substitute for the principal's leadership, the heroic image of the principalship lessened. Leadership became a function of the task to be performed in which task expertise and natural leadership ability superseded formal authority. This was a healthy and necessary change, but it left in question the role of the principal regarding leadership for school improvement.

THE NATURE OF LEADERSHIP FOR SCHOOL IMPROVEMENT

Rost's (1991) definition of leadership is a good beginning point for our discussion of leadership for school improvement.

"Leadership is an influence relationship among leaders and followers *who intend real changes that reflect their mutual purposes*" (italics added) (p. 102). In schools, leaders and followers influence each other toward some plan for school change that satisfies their collective vision.

Most research on the principal's school improvement role relates to leadership for a single innovation project. "What a principal does with one innovation does not necessarily predict what he or she will do with another one.... We cannot generalize from studies of single innovations. Related, and more fundamentally, the reality is that principals are not contending with individual innovations or even a series of innovations. They are in the business of attempting to manage multiple innovations" (Fullan, 1992, p. 83). Thus, expectations that the major leadership role of principals is in effecting single change projects result from an incomplete understanding of how principals influence school improvement and create an unrealistic portrayal of the principal's leadership role.

Fullan and others suggest a new conception of the leadership role for principals in school improvement. "We have begun to make the transition from the principal's role in influencing the implementation of specific innovations to the principal's role in leading changes in 'the school as an organization.' The implication is that we have to look deeper and more holistically at the principal and the school as an organization" (Fullan, 1992, pp. 84-85).

This leadership role is reflected in a new conception of school improvement. "As we look back on the 1970s and 1980s, we can appreciate that the research on effective schools helped us to understand that school improvement is not the result of fixing one or two elements in the school (say teacher supervision or improved inservice programs). Rather, we began to see that school improvement involves changing the culture of teacher isolation, changing the use of time and space, changing authority relationships, changing assessment procedures, changing the way schools work with parents, changing longstanding assumptions about teaching and learning" (Starratt, 1996, pp.

172–173). The principal's leadership role responds to these organizational changes.

INFLUENCING A SCHOOL IMPROVEMENT ENVIRONMENT

Leadership for school improvement is an influence relationship between leaders and followers to create a school improvement environment. This view of leadership goes well beyond simply persuading others to try a new innovation project. For example, instead of coaxing teachers into accepting a whole language approach in their classrooms, principals, within an influence relationship, persuade teachers to develop and commit to a climate of experimentation and collegiality.

This influence relationship is not simply a series of managerial actions. School effectiveness strategies generally encourage the principal to monitor instruction, adjust standard operating procedures, and obtain resources. However, by themselves these actions are good management but not leadership. However, if they are used to influence others to commit to a climate of change, they become powerful leadership tools. As we will see in the last section of this chapter, these managerial actions can be effective in persuading and supporting others to develop and maintain a school improvement environment.

Leadership for school improvement is too complex to involve only the principal. Teachers and students co-construct classroom learning environments. Parents facilitate or hinder norms and expectations of learning and teaching. It is unrealistic to suggest that principals can solely construct a school improvement environment. But it is inappropriate to assume that the principal has no relevant role to play in school improvement. Influencing others to cooperate in the development of a climate that supports transformative change is not only realistic but highly relevant.

Principals exercise leadership by means of three types of actions: bureaucratic, cultural, and educational. In this section we identify and briefly discuss these three and return to them in the final section to discuss leadership methods for school improvement.

BUREAUCRATIC ACTIONS

Five bureaucratic actions are illustrative of the principal's leadership role in school improvement: (1) obtaining resources; (2) providing encouragement and recognition; (3) adjusting standard operating procedures; (4) monitoring the improvement effort; and (6) handling disturbances (Heller and Firestone, 1995). Although some of these actions may be performed by the central office, e.g., resources, or by teachers, e.g., encouragement to each other, several may be most appropriately performed by the principal, e.g., adjusting standard operating procedures and handling disturbances.

As discussed earlier, these actions become leadership tools only as they are used to influence others to create and maintain an effective school improvement. For example, by adjusting standard operating procedures involving scheduling preparation periods, principals can encourage teachers to collaborate on new models of teaching and learning. Using this bureaucratic tool as a power resource, principals can make the school improvement environment more conducive to change.

CULTURAL ACTIONS

Besides bureaucratic actions, leadership for school improvement involves cultural actions. "...if the overall climate for innovation does not exist throughout the whole organization—a readiness to readjust in response to the changes that use of the innovation will require—it is highly unlikely that even the best ideas will reach the...mainstream" (Kanter, 1983, pp. 278-279). In Chapter 3, we described leadership in creating, maintaining, and changing school culture. The principal's influence in these areas produces an environment not only for experimenting with a single change project but committing to experimentation as a way of life in the school.

Beyond creating a shared vision that contributes to building an environment for school improvement, the cultural area of leadership also involves helping followers see efficacy in their school improvement efforts. "Administering an effective community implies a *cultural* activity by the educational administrator, namely, developing a communal sense of self-efficacy. With the experience of success in collaborative efforts, teachers develop a group sense of 'can do'.... The faculty and, indeed, the students and parents, grow to believe that they can solve their problems. They grow to believe that if they set a goal for themselves, they can achieve it" (Starratt, 1996, p. 174). In their ten-year study of effective and ineffective schools, Teddlie and Stringfield (1993) found that "the cultural connections that principals create also differ between the two groups of schools. In the less effective schools, norms of distance and laissez-faire indifference prevail; in the more effective schools, norms of interactive professional relationships are more common" (p. 168).

EDUCATIONAL ACTIONS

More recently another set of actions within the leadership role have been applied to school improvement. Instead of viewing learning as something that occurs only with students in the classroom, proponents of "learning organizations" suggest the importance of educating all constituents of the organization. " ... leaders in learning organizations are responsible for *building organizations* where people are continually expanding their capabilities to shape their future—that is, leaders are responsible for learning" (Senge, 1990, p. 9). The principal influences the school improvement environment by using expertise and inspiration to persuade others to test their models of teaching and learning and consider alternative models.

The principal is in an especially significant position to make apparent the mental models that followers and leaders use to understand current reality. By being aware of the larger organizational and environmental realities of the school, the principal can surface the assumptions that school constituents hold about the school's response to its external environment. "These mental pictures of how the world works have a significant influence on how we perceive problems and opportunities, identify courses of action, and make choices" (Senge, 1990, p. 12). These problem-finding and problem-solving capabilities, instead of being possessed only by the leader, are encouraged and developed in followers. They enable school constituents to understand current reality and develop visions for the future.

These three types of leadership actions assume a new conception of the principal's leadership role that is both relevant and realistic. Although teacher leaders can perform some of these responsibilities and central office administrators may perform others, principals are in the best position to provide the combination of these elements necessary to create an environment for school improvement. Such an environment goes beyond a single project to establish a new way of looking at teaching and learning, experimentation, collaboration, and organizational learning.

Principals can influence other leaders and followers to take actions to create such an environment and can influence the leadership capacities of others. By using such power resources as expertise, e.g., understanding and communicating the mental models that trap their perceptions of problems and opportunities, principals can influence students, teachers, parents, and community members to invest and participate in an environment that envisions substantive school change.

THE PARTICIPANTS OF
LEADERSHIP FOR SCHOOL IMPROVEMENT

Nowhere is it more evident that leadership involves both leaders and followers than in school improvement efforts. Numerous change studies, including the Rand studies of implementation (Berman and McLaughlin, 1978), encourage the involvement of the principal but recognize that others can act as leadership substitutes and that followers play a critical role in achievement. In this section we identify the roles of leaders and followers in school improvement and a specific leadership role of principals.

LEADERS' AND FOLLOWERS' ROLES

School improvement, like the other elements of school leadership that we have treated thus far, needs both leaders and followers to be successful. Kouzes and Posner (1987) maintain that while leaders are pioneers, they "need not always be the creators, or originators of new products or work processes. In fact, it is as likely that they are not. Product innovations tend to come from customers, vendors, and line employees. Process innovations tend to come from people doing the work....The leader's primary contribution is in the recognition of good ideas, the support of these ideas, and the willingness to challenge the system in order to get new products, processes, and services adopted. In this sense, it might be more accurate to call them early adopters of innovation" (p. 8). Creating an environment in which ideas are welcomed, developed, and supported is a relevant leadership role. Leaders influence followers as to the resources they secure, the inspiration they contribute, and the expertise they provide in considering new ways to look at organizational reality and future possibilities.

Yet followers also influence leaders. Followers provide the effort and commitment to carry out the change that determines the effectiveness. The Rand studies (Berman and McLaughlin, 1978) showed how projects are adapted through the implementation process at the classroom level. Followers also influence leaders in terms of their ideas regarding direction and purpose that provide the stimulus for reconsidering and/or creating shared visions. Finally, followers' observations and experiences may provoke the leader to consider the appropriateness of old mental models and the possibilities of new ones.

PRINCIPAL AS LEADER OF LEADERS FOR SCHOOL IMPROVEMENT

Beyond the leadership roles we have previously discussed, principals serve as leaders of leaders. Both inside and outside educational organizations, the use of teaming and more democratic leadership strategies are being used. Principals who enact their roles in rigid ways that limit the leadership of teams of teachers, students, and parents will have increasing difficulty influencing others. However, principals who see their roles as leaders of leaders can exert strong influence to create powerful school improvement environments.

The principal may follow the lead of teachers and parents who provide the disconfirming information regarding the effectiveness of current school improvement strategies. Still, principals have a leader role to play in school improvement. The principal as leader acts as a *teacher*, but this does not "mean leader as authoritarian expert whose job it is to teach people the 'correct' view of reality. Rather, it is about helping everyone in the organization, oneself included, to gain more insightful views of current reality" (Senge, 1990, p. 11). Principals as leaders of leaders serve in a teaching role to influence teachers, students, parents, and the community to reflect on their ways of understanding the purpose of schools and the nature of teaching and learning that opens them to new considerations of what schools can do. By providing such a learning environment, principals can lead others to be leaders of new school improvement conceptions.

ILLUSTRATION

Principal James Nelson and the faculty at Longview Alternative School together concluded that their alternative school had to approach teaching and learning differently than the traditional high school setting. The parents who wanted a more conventional school did not accept this approach. Among other things, they were uncomfortable with the lack of structure, e.g., open classrooms and outdoor education, and many global learning opportunities afforded the students.

The principal and key teacher leaders have spent considerable time each year meeting with parents in a variety of school settings. During these meetings, the principal engaged the parents in reflecting on the ways knowledge and learning have changed since they were in school and on the variety of new teaching/learning strategies available today. In a sense, he was helping to break down established parental paradigms and create new visions of teaching and learning to develop a learning community among the parents and newly hired teachers.

THE LOCATION OF
LEADERSHIP FOR SCHOOL IMPROVEMENT

Leadership for school improvement involves the active involvement of principals as leaders in external and internal spheres.

LEADERSHIP IN THE INTERNAL SPHERE

The internal environmental responsibility of leaders is critical in order for school improvement to occur. Considering and investing in school improvement within an internal environment in which collaboration and experimentation are encouraged is very different from what occurs in an internal environment where jealousy and fear of failure are encouraged. Although some single change innovations may "get through" in these negative environments, they will be short-lived and may even discourage future change projects. However, if the principal as leader can influence followers in the development of a climate where risk taking is encouraged, reflection is valued, and collaboration is rewarded, school improvement can become a natural and consistent feature of everyday school life.

Two essential features of principal leadership in the internal sphere influence other leaders and followers to create a school improvement environment. First, working with staff, students, and parents to identify the ways they view current reality—the assumptions and models they accept but rarely acknowledge that structure teaching and learning—is a critical responsibility for principals inside the school. If these assumptions remain unacknowledged, it is likely that school improvement projects will do little more than tinker with teaching and learning. Yet if these assumptions are recognized by staff, students, and parents, the possibilities for improving the learning environment are infinite.

Second, principals as leaders help internal constituents to think "systemically" about what happens in and to the school and why. This involves being aware of how teaching and learning influence, and are influenced by other activities within the school, e.g., maintenance and food service. In this way the classroom is connected to the larger school; teacher to teachers; student to students, etc.

In addition, systemic thinking enables those in the internal environment to understand how external factors influence and are influenced by the internal environment. Understanding the influence of the community, and the larger society becomes a vital component in refashioning teaching and learning.

ILLUSTRATION

Horace Mann Elementary School recently had faculty, staff, and some parents involved in strategic planning for the school. The custodians, secretaries, and food service personnel were delighted to become part of the planning and contributed significantly to the strategies. Susan O'Toole, the principal, claimed the head custodian took on a different role since the planning began. He is now regarded as a key member of the instructional team, a role he never considered before being included in the planning. Likewise, key parents have identified resources and individuals highly useful for implementing the plan.

Including these often excluded groups helped to highlight the assumptions that teachers and administrators did not recognize. Furthermore, custodians, secretaries, and parents had perspectives that expanded the systemic understanding to included noninstructional components of the school.

LEADERSHIP IN THE EXTERNAL SPHERE

Leadership for school improvement requires that principals are proactive in the external sphere for building a school improvement environment. Many resources that principals need to find for teachers and students are in the external environment and require that the principal persuasively express school needs and goals in order to acquire these resources.

The development of a shared vision of a school improvement environment requires external participation. Currently, communities are placing many demands on schools and are regarding schools with skepticism, if not cynicism. The day has long passed when principals can ignore community demands and perceptions.

Still, as we have noted in previous chapters, this leadership role does not mean simply being a sounding board for the community. If visions of school improvement are indeed collective visions, they must involve critical conversations among teachers, students, parents, administrators, and community members about teaching and learning.

Finally, leadership in the external environment involves influencing external constituents to surface their own assumptions about the nature of learning and the purposes of schools. Creating a "learning organization" must include both external constituents and internal constituents who can participate in creating and developing new school change models. The options are clear. Administrators and teachers can retain the old adversarial role with parents and communities and continue to find their visions disregarded and sabotaged by external interests. Or they can collaborate with parents and community members in a joint effort to understand each other's assumptions about schools and find their collective visions powerful engines for creating school environments that prepare students and families for the next century.

This is the struggle that Carolyn Duncan, in the vignette, is addressing with her grant proposal. She has mistakenly thought that it was up to her alone to lead the school community into new directions. When she does not involve others in the grant proposal, she is eliminating both ideas and commitment. Her burden has increased because she is carrying the major part of the load. Perhaps a better strategy is to develop the leadership of others—faculty, staff, parents, and students—to assume more of the responsibility for teaching and learning renewal. This does not merely mean Carolyn needs to delegate more, although that may eventually be part of it. More likely, Carolyn needs to enter a different kind of relationship with these groups and create a growing and learning environment. This is especially important with the teachers but also vital for the entire community. The relationship needs to be built upon mutual trust and understanding so that all ideas are respected and everyone feels a part of the organization and its growth.

THE PURPOSE OF
LEADERSHIP FOR SCHOOL IMPROVEMENT

In Rost's (1991) definition, the purpose of leadership is clear: "Leadership is an influence relationship among leaders and followers who *intend real changes that reflect their mutual purposes*" (italics added) (p. 102). Three points about the purpose of leadership for school improvement are evident from this definition. First, leaders and followers intend change, i.e., they see change as a continuing process, and they want certain changes in the way schools provide instruction. If this purpose is only the leader's, no leadership exists. Both leaders and followers must acknowledge the need for improvement in the achievement of their instructional goals.

Second, the changes must be substantive and transforming. Tinkering around the edges does not pass as real change. As we have acknowledged earlier, principal leadership is less evident in single innovation projects, possibly because the changes tend to be piecemeal instead of substantive and transforming. Leadership for school improvement involves changing the school environment so that leaders and followers are willing to consider perhaps radical, but certainly substantive, changes for the school.

Third, leadership for change focuses on the mutual purposes of leaders and followers. Rost maintains that this mutuality is forged in the noncoercive influence relationship. As principals, teachers, students, parents, and community members come together they forge shared purposes about school changes that meet their various needs. "The ultimate test of practical leadership is the realization of intended, real change that meets people's enduring needs." (Burns, 1978, p. 461).

What is the content of the purpose of leadership for school improvement? The easy answer is "more effective schools." We suggest there is a richer and longer-term purpose. Leadership for school improvement leads toward creating an environment that supports human growth in and for community (Dewey, 1900; Crow and Slater, 1996). The most critical purpose of principal leadership is to lead followers toward the creation of a school environment where adults and children grow. Leaving adults out of this learning environment ultimately impoverishes the environment for students. If adults are not learning and growing, the chances are very good that students are not as well.

However, this growth is not a simple individualistic endeavor. Principals are not leading followers toward the creation of a collection of separate individuals looking out for themselves. They influence other leaders and followers to create a climate where individual growth occurs within community contexts (both internal and external) and for the community's benefit. The current emphasis on individualism at the expense of community (Bellah et al., 1985) serves no one, especially students.

THE METHODS OF LEADERSHIP FOR SCHOOL IMPROVEMENT

In this section we turn to the methods of leadership for school improvement. We will organize our discussion in terms of methods related to the three functions of the leadership role identified earlier: bureaucratic, cultural, and educational.

BUREAUCRATIC METHODS OF LEADERSHIP

These leadership methods relate to the formal actions that principals take within the school to support an environment of educational improvement. Although an unusual place to start, the negative will suggest the role that principals can, but should not, play if they wish to build and maintain a school improvement setting. Kanter (1983) identifies ten "rules for stifling innovation."

+ Regard any new idea from below with suspicion— because it's new, and because it's from below.

+ Insist that people who need your approval to act first go through several other levels of management to get their signatures.

+ Ask departments or individuals to challenge and criticize each other's proposals. (That saves you the job of deciding; you just pick the survivor.)

+ Express your criticisms freely, and withhold your praise. (That keeps people on their toes.) Let them know they can be fired at any time.

+ Treat identification of problems as signs of failure, to discourage people from letting you know when something in their area isn't working.
+ Control everything carefully. Make sure people count anything that can be counted frequently.
+ Make decisions to reorganize or change policies in secret, and spring them on people unexpectedly. (That also keeps people on their toes.)
+ Make sure that requests for information are fully justified, and make sure that it is not given out to managers freely. (You don't want data to fall into the wrong hands.)
+ Assign to lower-level managers, in the name of delegation and participation, responsibilities for figuring out how to cut back, lay off, move people around, or otherwise implement threatening decisions you have made. And get them to do it quickly.
+ And above all, never forget that you, the higher-ups, already know everything important about this business.

Kanter's ten "rules" suggest that hierarchies, monitoring systems, and even delegation can be used to suppress innovation and change.

However, other bureaucratic methods can be used to influence an environment of change. The work of Firestone and his colleagues (Firestone and Corbett, 1988; Heller and Firestone, 1995) identifies several of these methods.

+ Obtaining resources
+ Adjusting standard operating procedures
+ Monitoring improvement efforts
+ Minimizing interruptions

Resources, such as slack time for teachers, students, and parents to collaborate; money; and clerical help provide power resources to influence school improvement efforts. Principals' leadership in securing resources also sends the message that change is valued not only in words but in actions.

ILLUSTRATION

After the faculty at Thomas Jefferson High School began restructuring in a conventional sense, they soon realized they did not have the time or the resources to continue. Teaching all day and then meeting in the late afternoons for planning was exhausting and actually detrimental to the planning process.

Principal Jim Buchanan recognized that faculty needed released time to meet and plan during the day. He developed strategies to release individual departments to meet together and to enable the entire faculty to meet regularly, for several hours at a time. Jim secured the cooperation of a local university education department to send college students who were prospective secondary teachers to the high school to act as substitutes. These college students taught classes while the department faculty were at a planning retreat.

To create time for the entire faculty to meet together, the principal designed a scheduling model that extended class time four days a week so that one afternoon each week students were released early. The school did this for an entire year and developed an award winning restructuring plan that was well received by the entire community. The principal worked with the bureaucratic elements to obtain the needed changes. In a concrete way, faculty saw their principal put his words of renewal into action.

Reducing interruptions, especially from the system, facilitates a climate in which change can grow with as few disturbances as possible. "Too often principals revamp discipline policies at the same time they revise lesson plan formats; superintendents standardize curriculums and concurrently initiate special reading projects in all academic subjects; state agencies launch new testing programs while altering graduate requirements and curriculum standards" (Firestone and Corbett, 1988, p. 330).

Reducing interruptions involves maintaining initiative and control. Schools cannot be environments of school improvement if they are constantly bombarded by new and changing improvement projects. Communicating to external constituents the vision of school improvement efforts, especially when these external constituents have been included in the goal-setting activities, ensures a less interrupted environment for school change to occur.

CULTURAL METHODS OF LEADERSHIP

Clearly, if the most appropriate and reasonable role for principals is in influencing the creation and maintenance of an environment for school improvement, the importance of cultural methods of leadership should be evident. We identify three kinds of cultural methods which principals as leaders can use for school improvement.

+ Inspiring vision and focus
+ Enabling and encouraging
+ Modeling attitudes of change

INSPIRING A SHARED VISION AND FOCUS

The primary cultural action that principals can take as leaders for school improvement is constructing and reinforcing vision and focus. Inspiring a shared vision means that principals lead students, teachers, parents, administrators, and community members to look at both the future and the present, i.e., what larger picture integrates various change projects. Schools, like many other organizations, have a tendency to create change projects without an integrating vision or focus. The principal provides the inspiration and guidance to create a collective picture of the future that provides the rationale for change projects and helps create an ongoing school change environment.

"In some ways leaders live their lives backward. They see pictures in their minds' eyes of what the results will look like even before they have started their projects, much as an architect draws a blueprint or an engineer builds a model....But visions seen only by leaders are insufficient to create an organized movement or a significant change.... A person with no followers is not a leader, and people will not become followers until they accept a vision as their own. You cannot command commitment, you can only inspire it" (Kouzes and Posner, 1987, p. 9).

Fullan (1992) provides three specific suggestions for principals regarding vision: focus on priorities, especially curriculum and instruction; "start small, think big;" and concentrate on the fundamental, such as the school's professional culture (pp. 88-90). He maintains that the best means for concentrating on the fundamental is through curriculum changes.

ENABLING AND ENCOURAGING OTHERS

Kanter (1983) calls for leaders to create a "culture of pride, climate of success." Such an environment leads to change because people "feel they belong to a meaningful entity and can realize cherished values by their contributions" (p. 149). This kind of culture provides "a self-reinforcing upward cycle—performance stimulating pride stimulating performance—and is especially important for innovation" (p. 151).

One strategy principals can use is to facilitate a sense of self-efficacy among teachers. Teaching is an isolated activity with a paucity of frequent, apparent rewards (Lortie, 1975), especially in contemporary schools. Principals who are aware of what teachers and students are doing, knowledgeable of their successes, and able to communicate these successes sensitively to them can make an immeasurable contribution to a "culture of pride, climate of success" in school improvement. "Publicizing successes, praising initiative, calling people together to discuss common concerns, engaging in problem naming and problem finding, and providing institutional support for group initiatives will help to create a culture of self-efficacy" (Starratt, 1996, pp. 174–175).

Encouraging others to persevere is essential to ensuring self-efficacy. "The climb to the top is arduous and long. People become exhausted, frustrated, and disenchanted. They often are tempted to give up. Leaders must encourage the heart of their followers to carry on" (Kouzes and Posner, 1987, p. 12).

Earlier we wrote about a school whose faculty had given up on site-based management. Perhaps the faculty gave up too soon. When additional tasks were assigned and site-based decision making was obviously going to be more work for the faculty, the principal needed to take on the "coaching" role and encourage others to persist. Without that kind of leadership, renewal and change will be hot for a season but soon turn cold.

MODELING CHANGE

The third set of actions that principals as leaders can take in developing a school improvement environment is to model certain characteristics and behaviors. Throughout this book, one of the primary leadership methods we have identified has been *attending*. What principals pay attention to reinforces and changes culture, inspires vision, and promotes school improvement. The Teddlie and Stringfield study (1993) of school effects, cited earlier, clearly provides evidence that the things principals pay attention to, e.g., children's learning, hiring the best teachers, and higher order thinking skills, influence the kinds of effective schools that exist. This is not to suggest that the principal's attention is both necessary and sufficient for school improvement. Rather, what principals pay attention to by their behavior and talk sends a message to students, teachers, parents, and others that school improvement is important enough to affect the way principals carry out their responsibilities.

Fullan (1992) suggests that principals need to "practice fearlessness and other forms of risk-taking" (p. 90). In answering the question of how some principals get away with certain actions, he replies, "It is somewhat superficial to say, but nonetheless true, that 'they just do it'" (p. 90). Besides being careful not to punish risk taking in followers, principals can encourage it by modeling risk taking themselves.

EDUCATIONAL METHODS OF LEADERSHIP

Beyond the bureaucratic and cultural, methods relating to the educating role of principals as leaders for school improvement are important. We describe three such methods.

> ◆ Begin with self
> ◆ Surface and test mental models
> ◆ Promote systems thinking

BEGIN WITH SELF

Before principals can influence students, teachers, parents, other administrators, and community members to develop learning skills for school improvement, they must reflect on their own practice. "The starting point from the individual principal's point of view should be a reflection on whether his or her own conception of the role of the principal has built-in limitations regarding change. Principals within the same system operating in almost identical circumstances will work with change or avoid it, depending on *their* conception of the role. Just as teachers' sense of efficacy is important in bringing about school improvement, so is the principal's—perhaps more significant because it affects *the whole organization*" (Fullan, 1992, p. 87).

Principal preparation and inservice programs are increasingly turning to reflective practice as a tool for changing principal role conception (Osterman and Kottkamp, 1993; Hart, 1993). If principals reflect on their own conceptions of the role, the purposes of schooling, and the nature of teaching and learning, they not only surface their own assumptions about school improvement problems and opportunities, but identify likely ones for teachers to consider.

Often principals need to initiate reflection with others. Dialogue is a form of reflection. Consider the vignette. Carolyn and Richard have talked about schools and leadership during their flight to a conference in New Orleans. This dialogue has initiated considerable reflection for both educators. In fact, we hope to illustrate that such dialogue has promoted better leadership through reflection. John Dewey is quoted as saying, "...While we cannot learn or be taught to think, we do have to learn how to think well, especially how to acquire the general habit of reflecting." Both Richard and Carolyn have improved their leadership before attending the conference, by the simple act of dialogue with a colleague and promoting self-reflection.

Dewey suggests that we develop a general habit of reflecting, which is critically needed for school leaders who often live and work in hectic schedules that promote isolation.

SURFACE AND TEST MENTAL MODELS

Administrators, teachers, students, parents, and community members assume particular models regarding change, the nature of teaching and learning, the purpose of schooling, and a variety of other critical features of school practice. Frequently these models are untested and unacknowledged, but still influence the kinds of change projects assumed to be "doable" and "appropriate." Before effective environments for school improvement can be developed, these models must be surfaced and tested. The principal is the most obvious leader to encourage other leaders and followers to acknowledge and test their assumptions.

There are four methods (suggested by Senge, 1990) that principals can use in leading themselves and others to surface mental models:

+ Acknowledge leaps of abstractions,
+ Balance inquiry and advocacy,
+ Distinguish espoused theory from theory in use; and
+ Recognize and defuse defensive behaviors.

First, principals need to help themselves and others acknowledge the way they confuse generalization with observable data. Frequently, without any reliable data to support it, individuals generalize about parents' commitment to their children, students' learning motivation, and teachers' commitment to teaching. Such generalizations do little to accomplish change or create environments that support school improvement.

Second, principals can encourage balancing inquiry and advocacy. Due to the urgency of students' needs, principals may advocate new ideas without sufficient inquiry. Grabbing the latest fad and packaged human relations or curriculum model without sufficient investigation of how these may work in a particular setting does not promote school improvement.

The Accelerated Schools project promotes the notion of inquiry as a central requirement of change. In the example used earlier in this book, Peter Lucke, an elementary principal, submits his own ideas for change to the inquiry process. While he admits this is frustrating at times, the inquiry process is valuable since it reinforces the importance of understanding and inquiry as a prerequisite for school change.

WHEN LEADERS ARE ADVOCATING CHANGE, THEY NEED TO BE ABLE TO:

♦ explain reasoning and data that lead to the view;

♦ encourage others to test their view; and

♦ encourage others to provide different views.

WHEN LEADERS ARE INQUIRING INTO ANOTHER'S VIEW, THEY NEED TO:

♦ actively seek to understand their view, rather than simply restate their own view, and

♦ make their attributions about the other and the other's view explicit.

From Senge, P.M. (1990). The leader's new work: Building learning organizations. *MIT Sloan Management Review*, (Feb.), p. 14.

The third method that can encourage leaders and followers to acknowledge their mental models is to help them distinguish those theories they espouse from those they actually use. Principals as leaders help followers make this distinction, in a psychologically safe environment, where surfacing our theories in use is vital to creating an environment for school improvement.

The fourth method involves recognizing and defusing defensive behaviors. Most of us package our ideas and visions with ego investment, so that if our ideas are questioned or criticized, we protect ourselves from embarrassment and threat. This hinders clarity and depth of inquiry and prevents our school change models from being adequately assessed. Principals as leaders for school improvement influence others to recognize and avoid defensiveness that prevents ideas and models from being adequately understood and tested.

ILLUSTRATION

Charles Shackett, principal of Highland High School in Salt Lake City, used a unique and inspirational method of introducing a strategic planning session with the faculty, staff and representative parents. At the beginning of the session, which was the first of many to follow, he introduced the planning process. As he began his remarks, he took off his sports coat. A few minutes into his presentation, he took off his shirt and tie. He then continued with his presentation, taking off one item of clothing at a time until he was down to his boxer shorts.

His final remarks, which left an impression not soon forgotten, were, "I have nothing to hide. I have nothing up my sleeves. I just want us all to go through a strategic planning process without thinking that the principal has a hidden agenda. I hope to have impressed upon you that I have no investment in my own pride that should interfere with our planning this year."

Charles Shackett's dramatic introduction to strategic planning exemplified commitment and daring. This established a climate for his leadership that he has exploited by consciously adhering to the four principles set down in this section.

PROMOTE SYSTEMS THINKING

Throughout this book we have encouraged thinking about leadership roles from both internal and external perspectives. One feature of this approach is to think systemically, that is to consider the interrelationships between internal and external environments that exist in school organizations. If the principal is to exercise a relevant leadership role in establishing and maintaining a school change environment, systemic thinking is critical. For example, a climate that facilitates teaching and learning, without considering the influence of parents and the community, ignores a major source of ideas and values that affect learning.

Based on Senge (1990), we have adapted several features of systems thinking which are crucial for leadership in establishing a school improvement environment. First, seeing interrelationships and processes is necessary. Instead of viewing school improvement as a series of change projects, viewing it as integration of changes is critical. Instead of understanding school improvement from a snapshot perspective, it is important to understand it as an ongoing systemwide process involving a variety of people, tasks, times, places, and ideas.

Second, principals need to influence leaders and followers to move beyond blame. Instead of accusing others of preventing or hindering school improvement, look at systemwide structures and processes that discourage attitudes of change. Furthermore, "avoid symptomatic solutions" (Senge, 1990, p. 15). The urgency of schooling sometimes encourages individuals to short cut inquiry and focus on the symptoms rather than the problems and opportunities of school improvement. Engaging in problem finding and problem solving is critical in creating an environment that supports substantive, transformative change in schools.

Third, principals need to develop in themselves and others the skill of focusing on areas of high leverage. Rather than attempt to change all areas of instructional practice, the principal as leader should influence school constituents to focus on those areas where change is most possible and where change will make the most difference for school improvement. This will vary with each school and system. Nevertheless, it is the principal's responsibility to know the system and to communicate and develop that understanding with followers so that decisions can have the most effect.

By maintaining that the principal's most critical role is to influence the establishment and maintenance of an environment for school improvement, we have constructed a realistic and relevant view of the principal's leadership role. Not only is there a role for principals as leaders for school improvement, but this role is critical for the future development of schools as environments that enable human growth in and for community.

REFLECTIVE VIGNETTE

The flight to New Orleans was starting its descent. The flight attendant gathered the empty cups from Carolyn and Richard. Richard asked Carolyn why she had gotten into education. She related to him how she had always loved going to school and had played teacher in her room when she was younger. "I took my first job teaching English in a combined junior-senior high school in a small Colorado town. I was young and single and wanting adventure and will never forget that town or that school. I remember at Christmas we had a pageant that was a big deal to this small town. Everybody who was anybody came to it. We would pack the school gymnasium and every kid from elementary through high school and every teacher had some part. At the end of the pageant the local grocery store brought in frozen turkeys and gave every teacher one. I often think of that community and that school and long for the return to that sense of community that existed there."

"That sounds like a wonderful place. Why did you ever leave?" asked Richard.

"The district consolidated the senior high school into a larger high school in the next town. I was one of the newer teachers so I got RIF'd. It was time for me to move on anyway. I never really planned to spend my career there. It was a wonderful experience while it lasted."

"Have you ever thought of trying to get that same sense of community in your high school?"

"Totally impossible!" was Carolyn's quick response. "Things are different than they were twenty years ago. The city is different from the small town. The kids are different. Teachers have a different agenda. I don't even think there is anything the same."

"I wonder if most teachers, parents, and students want that sense of community in their schools much as you found in that small Colorado school? As our school has gotten larger due to the year round plan, I think teachers and parents feel more distance between them and the school."

The seat belt sign came on with a short announcement by the flight attendant to prepare for landing. "I wish we could talk more," Carolyn said. "Our conversation today has been very helpful to me. I feel invigorated just to have someone who will talk about the same things I am interested in. It is funny how we principals do not have too many opportunities to talk with each other. "

Richard responded, "You are right. There have been times when I have felt a need to talk but there was no one there. I am quite interested in your final proposal for the technology grant. Perhaps you could telephone me sometime and tell me how you come out with it."

"I'll even do better than that," said Carolyn. "If you would like, how about paying a visit to Central High some afternoon? We could escape for a brief lunch and then I could show you around the school. We could discuss the final proposal before I send it in. I need a good reviewer to give me some last minute feedback."

"I would like that very much. Here is my card with my telephone and e-mail address. Please call me when you are ready and I will be glad to drive over and visit with you."

SELF-REFLECTION ACTIVITIES

- ♦ In your experience have you found that parents, students and teachers want the sense of community that Richard described? Can schools in urban and suburban areas and consolidated schools create the kind of community that Carolyn described in her small-town school?

- ♦ Carolyn claims that a sense of community is not likely to occur in her school because times have changed, students have changed, and teachers have a different agenda. Is this true for your school? How does this affect change in your school?

♦ What can you do to encourage rather than discourage attitudes about change?

PEER-REFLECTION ACTIVITIES

♦ With a peer, discuss teachers in your school that often resist change. Why do they resist change? How can you and your peer as school principals help reduce this resistance?

♦ Reflect together on this statement: *Teaching is an isolated activity with a lack of frequent, apparent rewards.* How does this impede the development of an environment for change?

♦ Reflect together on how principals can reduce the isolation of teachers.

♦ Discuss with a peer the importance of a colleague with whom a principal can engage in reflective practice.

COURSE ACTIVITIES

♦ Consider this statement: *Learning is not something that occurs only with students; all constituents in an organization are involved with learning.* Discuss the kinds of learning that are important for principals, faculty, staff, and parents to enhance the school improvement environment.

♦ Distinguish between developing a learning environment as discussed in this chapter and developing the more traditional staff development programs.

♦ Consider Kanter's rules for stifling innovation on pages 111–112. Elicit from class discussion examples of each of the ten rules.

♦ Invite a rural school principal and an urban school principal to class. Ask them to discuss the ways they work toward developing a positive learning environment in their schools. Compare and contrast their experiences and views.

6

A LEADERSHIP ROLE FOR PRINCIPALS: REALISTIC AND RELEVANT

This book represents an attempt to define the principal's leadership role in ways that avoid the extreme conceptualizations which characterize the role as either sterile or heroic. In place of these extremes, we have argued for a leadership role for principals that meets criteria that can be characterized as realistic and relevant—one that neither assumes the principal is the sole leader in the school nor ignores the significant leadership role principals can play. This final chapter consists of two parts: a summary of the arguments for our position and a look to the future.

SUMMARY

The examination of the leadership role for principals began with a framework which permits an organization of knowledge from the authoritative literature and from practice. That framework includes five parts: nature, participants, location, purpose, and methods. In this section we apply our criteria of relevancy and reality to each part of the framework in highlighting the major features of the principal's leadership role.

THE NATURE OF LEADERSHIP

Leadership is an influence relationship between leaders and followers. Defining it in this way allows us to specify a role for principals that is both realistic and relevant. The complex and dynamic nature of schools and their environments requires leadership that goes beyond the work of one individual or one formal position. The principal exercises leadership as do teachers and others by influencing individuals. This influence occurs by using power resources such as expertise, charisma, interpersonal skills, negotiation, political clout, and rewards.

Defining leadership as an influence relationship acknowledges that instead of coercive power, leadership is more complex and transactional. The process of leaders and followers influencing each other to change a school culture, create a new collective vision for a school, and establish an environment to support school improvement is dynamic. A vibrant set of relationships has power because it stimulates ideas, obtains commitment to programs, and energizes individual performance.

This definition of leadership draws a distinction between leadership and management. If management behavior is used to influence others to follow a particular course or engage in developing a school improvement environment, this management behavior can be considered leadership. However, if it is performed only to run the school more smoothly, it is not leadership. This is not to discount the value of good management; rather, it is to distinguish management and leadership. This distinction enables us to identify a relevant role for principals—influencing others to create substantive and transformative change (Rost, 1991; Burns, 1978).

This view of leadership was then applied to the three areas of culture, vision, and change. First, principals play a significant role in influencing others to consider whether the school is successfully addressing its internal and external problems and by that whether it should change its values, beliefs, and assumptions. Second, principals influence others by creating a personal vision of what the school can be and by leading others to develop a collective vision toward which to work. Finally, principals play a significant leadership role in school improvement, namely, influencing others to develop and maintain an environment that supports substantive school change.

THE PARTICIPANTS OF LEADERSHIP

Leadership involves both leaders and followers. Rather than leadership being a permanent designation or confined to a formal role, it is a relationship involving the active participation of both followers and leaders. Principals, teachers, students, and parents may be either leaders or followers whose designation may change depending on the particular issue or problem. Followers play a relevant role in being willing to commit to cultural values, a particular vision, and a concept of change as well as being free to question leader actions and directions. Including all relevant individuals in the leadership relationship is more realistic in terms of how schools function and the way in which influence is generated and exercised. The principal clearly is not the only individual leading and influencing. In fact. at times, principals follow the lead of others.

Perhaps the principal's most relevant leadership role is as "leader of leaders" (Schlechty, 1990). Principals influence teachers, students, and parents to take on leader roles. Developing leadership potential in others is a crucial need in contemporary schools. If schools are too complex and exist in an environment that is too dynamic for leadership to be confined to the activities of one person, then someone needs to develop the potential in others to disperse leadership throughout the organization (Crow and Slater, 1996). As principals serve as leaders of leaders, they multiply the effect of their influence—not by cloning but by empowering.

Leaders and followers influence each other in maintaining and changing culture, developing a collective vision, and establishing a school improvement environment. The principal's leadership role is both realistic and relevant in these areas. Once established, a school culture influences the principal's actions as much or more than the principal influences the culture. Likewise, although principals should develop their own visions, they are not the only ones with visions for the school. As for change, research has shown that principals have limited influence on single change projects and thus we need to look beyond these projects for a more relevant role for principals.

Principals lead other leaders and followers in the school to "keep the faith" in terms of the current values, norms, and beliefs. However, when these values are ineffective in helping the school address its internal and external problems, principals influence others to acknowledge the disconfirming information and provide enough security to consider change. Principals also play a significant leadership role in influencing teachers, students, and parents to share their own visions and use these in constructing a collective vision for the school. Finally, principals influence others in establishing an environment for school improvement.

THE LOCATION FOR LEADERSHIP

Principals exercise leadership both inside and outside the school. No longer can principals simply influence insiders and expect to make a significant difference in the school. Acknowledging that leadership must confront both internal and external problems and environments also implies a realistic awareness of the leadership exerted by these individuals and forces both inside and outside the school. Besides teachers, students, and parents, external individuals, e.g., central office administrators, community leaders, government officials, and political interest groups, attempt to influence the principal to address their demands. Recognizing these dynamics allows us to place principal leadership in a realistic context where inside and outside leadership forces exist.

At the same time, these spheres of leadership permit the principal to exert considerable influence on schools and their environments. Reforms need to be systemic to be successful and lasting. Systemic change requires the recognition of the interrelationships of persons external to the school who affect school culture, vision, and change. Systemic change also requires the knowledge of how these external individuals can best interact with the internal environment to bring about positive results. Principals play a relevant leadership role by being in contact with these systemic forces and by having the opportunity to shape their perspectives on the school culture, vision, and change. This role also includes being able to bring them or their ideas into the internal environment in a productive manner. Instead of being simply a sounding board for community demands and concerns, the principal can become a major shaper of environmental values and expectations.

THE PURPOSE OF LEADERSHIP

The purpose of the influence relationship of leadership is to cause substantive and transformative change. Yet change does not exist to benefit the leader but rather to meet the mutual needs of both leaders and followers. Realistically, principals, in consort with teachers, students, parents, and community members, attempt to negotiate changes that meet their mutual needs. Fortunately for schools, change is not defined by one individual's needs or by the expectations of a particular role.

Principals play a relevant role in influencing others to bring about change. Beyond the direct influence concerning a particular vision of change, principals as leaders of leaders develop others' potential to bring their own visions and concerns into the negotiation process. This role need not reduce the principal's influence, but can multiply the effect of leadership throughout the organization—creating a more effective culture, vision, and change environment.

The purpose of leadership as influencing change also involves a content. Principals and other leaders and followers in schools work toward substantive change in culture, vision, and school improvement focused on *human growth in and for community*. Growth is not individualistic—that is, focused on the needs and potential of single individuals. Rather the focus is on the growth of all members of the school community as they study and work with mutual support in a community environment.

THE METHODS OF LEADERSHIP

The methods of leadership also exemplify our criteria of relevant and realistic. Throughout our examination of leadership, we have identified common, routine—and realistic—actions that principals can take to exert leadership. For example, attending to certain types of behavior, obtaining resources, and adjusting standard operating procedures are routine activities of a principal's everyday work. They are not heroic actions taken occasionally by an elite group of principals to inspire teachers, students, and parents to achieve some goal. On the contrary, they are realistic activities that any principal can and should do.

Nevertheless, what makes these methods leadership and therefore relevant for principals is that they are guided by an attempt to influence others to maintain or change school culture, develop a collective vision, and establish an environment to support school improvement. These routine activities take on significant proportions because they are focused and integrated toward some larger purpose.

Besides these routine behaviors, we have also identified symbolic methods that influence others, e.g., ceremonies, rituals, and stories. These methods inspire and encourage others to risk questioning their values and beliefs, contribute to a collective vision, and participate in establishing a school improvement environment. In so doing, they contribute to the principal's relevant leadership role in influencing others.

PRINCIPAL LEADERSHIP FOR THE FUTURE

We have defined principal leadership as being realistic and relevant, in terms of the contemporary contexts in which principals work. This definition is also valid for future settings that new and current principals will encounter. In this section, we apply our definition of the principal's leadership role to four features of future leadership environments.

BEYOND EFFECTIVE MANAGEMENT

In 1952, the University Council for Educational Administration (UCEA) conducted a study of principal preparation texts. That study found that the principal's role could be summarized as "opening the school in the fall, running the school during the school year, and closing the school in the spring." The principalship was essentially the practice of good scientific management. Today, we realize that effective management is no longer sufficient for schools. The exploding nature of technology, the changing qualities of the student population, and the intractable movement toward democratization and collective governance all require something beyond effective management (Odden, 1995). Although effective management will remain necessary, it will be conducted competently but almost unconsciously, i.e., it will cease to be considered a priority.

Management without leadership is now inappropriate, and will become unacceptable in future schools. A principal who cannot influence others and be influenced by others to question old models and risk trying new ones is bound for failure. Under such circumstances principals need to become competent in their management skills, but expert in the skills, identified throughout the book, relating to culture, vision, and change in schools.

Contemporary schools differ from past schools, and future schools will depart significantly from contemporary schools. Principal leadership will be the key in the necessary transformations which are already in formative stages. Success or failure will occur school by school as principals undertake the leadership that will be thrust upon them. We believe strongly that the keys to successful leadership for the school principal lie in the concepts, ideas, and principles set forth here.

SYSTEMIC LEADERSHIP

The boundaries between future schools and their environments will be harder to define. The distinction we have made between internal and external is increasingly an artifact of the past. Those who suggest that the principalship will eventually disappear, leaving teachers to lead schools, have ignored this boundary issue. The growing permeability of schools requires a principal, but it requires one that exercises leadership in a larger sphere— systemic leadership.

Systemic leadership will require that principals think of leadership as an influence relationship occurring throughout the system. Teachers, students, parents, district administrators, government officials, community members, and political interest groups will not decrease their exercise of leadership; rather, they will increase their attempts to influence the school to address their concerns. Teachers will demand and achieve more control over instructional matters. Parents will demand and get more choice and voice in school governance. Communities and governmental officials will demand schools to be more open to public scrutiny and more accountable.

Principals can provide a relevant leadership role if they are sensitive to concerns and issues of all stakeholders and lead in shaping values, beliefs, and assumptions accordingly. The principalship needs to become a force in the system in order for change to occur. Leadership actions contrast with simply defending the school against outside agitators and involve actively shaping the values and beliefs of all parts of the system. One may argue that this is what good principals have been doing for some time. Nevertheless, in the future, all principals will have to become adept at systemic leadership. This leadership role will be a necessary expectation rather than an example of exemplary performance.

FOCUSING ON LEADERSHIP RATHER THAN LEADERS

Future schools will be far more complex, and environments far more dynamic than contemporary schools and environments. Leadership is required that goes beyond a single individual or formal position. Principals need teachers, students, parents, community members, and others to work with them to exercise leadership in order to respond to opportunities and challenges.

This emphasis on leadership requires principals to be flexible and open to the leadership of others. Teaming, for example, may be called something else, but the democratization moves experienced in the past few years will continue and expand. A principal who is rigid and authoritarian will have trouble influencing others. However, the principal who is flexible and open to the potential of leadership in others will be able to influence schools to make substantive changes.

These circumstances require principals to develop the leadership potential of others. Instead of fearing that this will reduce their own influence, principals will need to focus on leadership rather than leaders. Increasing the leadership potential in the school multiples the possibilities for more vibrant school cultures, more transformative collective visions, and more exciting environments, in which adults **and** students can learn. The principal is an obvious person to direct attention and resources toward developing the leadership potential in the school.

LEADERSHIP FOR RESPONSIBILITY

Contemporary schools mirror contemporary society. The violence, hate, lack of responsibility, and other ills in evidence in the larger society have entered the school. Unless we find ways to develop more responsible adults, these forces will continue and escalate. Schools and their leaders are caught up in societal problems and need to take a proactive stance regarding the school's involvement with the external environment.

We have argued that the purpose of leadership is substantive change and in particular change to enhance human growth in and for community. Individualism as a primary, if not all consuming force, does no service to the society, especially its children. Principals can play a critical role in influencing teachers, students, parents, and community members to question the assumptions of individualism and risk attempts to try new models that generate cooperation, community and responsibility. By modeling behaviors that attend to human growth for and in community, by questioning old models of teaching and learning, and by supporting cultural community, principals are pivotal leaders in a central societal institution. Past assumptions held that schools change slowly and mirror society, that schooling changes the new generation which in turn, through education, will transform society over time. This assumption is no longer tenable.

CONCLUSION

The needs of leadership for the future begin with the principals and prospective principals of today. These individuals are or will be in positions to exercise leadership and develop the leadership potential of others to change cultures, develop collective visions, and establish school improvement environments that respond to these future demands. The beginning requires a realistic awareness of how influence develops in schools and a commitment and belief in a relevant role for principals in contemporary and future schools. Self-reflection, peer reflection, and formal training can move principals and prospective principals away from an "everything or nothing" dilemma to a realistic and relevant leadership role.

REFERENCES

CHAPTER 1: PRINCIPAL LEADERSHIP: EVERYTHING OR NOTHING

Baltzell, D.C., & Dentler, R.A. (1983). *Selecting American school principals: A source book for educators.* Washington, DC: U.S. Department of Education, National Institute of Education.

Barnard, C. (1948). *Organizations and management.* Cambridge, MA: Harvard University Press.

Barnard, C. (1938). *The functions of the executive.* Cambridge, MA: Harvard University Press.

Beck, L.G., & Murphy, J. (1993). *Understanding the principalship: Metaphorical themes from 1920–1990.* New York: Teachers College Press.

Blake, R.R., & Mouton, J.S. (1982). Management by grid principles as situationalism: Which? *Group and Organizational Studies, 7,* 207–210.

Blase, J. (1989). The micropolitics of the school: The everyday political perspective of teachers toward open school principals. *Educational Administration Quarterly, 24*(4), 377–407.

Burns, J.M. (1978). *Leadership.* New York: Harper and Row.

Callahan, R.E. (1962). *Education and the cult of efficiency: A study of the social forces that have shaped the administration of public schools.* Chicago: University of Chicago Press.

Crow, G.M. (1990). Central office influence on the principal's relationship with teachers. *Administrators Notebook, 34*(1), 1–4.

Fiedler, F.E. (1964). A contingency model of leadership effectiveness. In L. Berkowitz (Ed.), *Advances in experimental social psychology.* New York: Academic Press.

Fiedler, F.E. (1967). *A theory of leadership effectiveness.* New York: McGraw-Hill.

French, J.R.P., Jr., & Raven, B.H. (1959). The bases of social power. In D. Cartwright (Ed.). *Studies in social power.* 150–167. Ann Arbor, MI.: Institute for Social Research, University of Michigan.

Gardner, J. W. (1965). The antileadership vaccine. *Annual Report of the Carnegie Corporation of New York.* New York, 12.

Greenfield, W.D. (1977). Administrative candidacy: A process of new role learning—Part I. *Journal of Educational Administration, 15*(1), 30–48.

Greenfield, W.D. (1983). Career dynamics of educators: research and policy issues. *Educational Administration Quarterly, 19*(2), 5-26.

Hart, A.W. (1993). *Principal succession: Establishing leadership in schools.* Albany, NY: State University of New York Press.

Hart, A.W., & Bredeson, P.V. (1996). *The principalship. A theory of professional learning and practice.* New York: McGraw-Hill.

Howard, A., & Bray, D.W. (1988). *Managerial lives in transition: Advancing age and changing times.* New York: Guilford Press.

Katz, D., & Kahn, R. L. (1966, 1978). *The social psychology of organizations.* New York: Wiley.

Kerr, J., & Jermier, J.M. (1978). Substitutes for leadership: Their meaning and measurement. *Organizational Behavior and Human Performance, 22,* 375–403.

Leithwood, K.A. (1994). Leadership for school restructuring. *Educational Administration Quarterly, 30*(4), 498–518.

Leithwood, K.A., & Jantzi, D. (1990). Transformational leadership: How principals can help reform school cultures. *School Effectiveness and School Improvement, 1*(4), 249–280.

Leithwood, K.A., & Steinbach, R. (1991). Indicators of transformational leadership in the everyday problem-solving of school administrators. *Journal of Personnel Evaluation in Education 4,* 221–244.

Leithwood, K.A., & Steinbach, R. (1993). Total quality leadership: Expert thinking plus transformation practice. *Journal of Personnel Evaluation in Education 7*(4), 311–338.

Likert, R. (1961). *New patterns of management.* New York: McGraw-Hill.

Likert, R. (1967). *The human organization: Its management and value.* New York: McGraw-Hill.

Lortie, D.C. (1975). *Schoolteacher: A sociological study.* Chicago: University of Chicago Press.

McCauley, C.D., & Lombardo, M.M. (1990). Benchmarks: An instrument for diagnosing managerial strengths and weaknesses. In K. E. Clark and M. B. Clark (Eds.), *Measures of leadership*, 535–545. West Orange, NJ: Leadership Library of America.

Milstein, M.M., Bobroff, B.M. & Restine, L.N. (1991). *Internship programs in educational administration.* New York: Teachers College Press.

Murphy, J. (Ed.). (1993). *Preparing tomorrow's school leaders: Alternative designs.* University Park, PA: University Council for Educational Administration.

Murphy, J. (1988). Methodological, measurement, and conceptual problems in the study of instructional leadership. *Education Evaluation and Policy Analysis, 10*(2), 117–139.

Odden, A.R. (1995). *Educational leadership for American schools.* New York: McGraw-Hill.

Ogawa, R.T., & Bossert, S.T. (1995). Leadership as an organizational quality. *Educational Administration Quarterly, 31*(2), 224–243

Pitner, N.J. (1986). Substitutes for principal leader behavior: An exploratory study. *Educational Administration Quarterly, 22,* 23–42.

Rost, J.C. (1991). *Leadership for the twenty-first century.* New York: Praeger.

Rowan, B., & Denk, C.E. (1984). Management succession, school socioeconomic context, and basic skills achievement. *American Educational Research Journal, 21*(3), 517–537.

Schein, E.H. (1992). *Organizational culture and leadership.* (2nd ed). San Francisco: Jossey-Bass Publishers.

Stahl, M. J. (1983). Achievement, power and managerial motivation: Selecting managerial talent with the job choice exercise. *Personal Psychology, 36,* 775–789.

Stogdill, R.M., Goode, O.S., & Day, D.R. (1962). New leader behavior description subscales. *Journal of Psychology, 54*, 259–269.

Tannenbaum, A.S. (1962). Control in organizations: Individual adjustment and organizational performance. *Administrative Science Quarterly, 7*, 236–257.

Thompson, J.D. (1967). *Organizations in action.* New York: McGraw-Hill.

Tyack, D., & Hansot, E. (1982). *Managers of virtue. Public school leadership in America, 1820–1980.* New York: Basic Books.

Yukl, G. (1994). *Leadership in organizations, (3rd. ed.).* Englewood Cliffs, NJ: Prentice Hall.

Yukl, G., & Falbe, C.M. (1990). Influence tactics in upward, downward, and lateral influence attempts. *Journal of Applied Psychology, 75*, 132–140.

Zaleznik, A. (1989). *The managerial mystic.* New York: Edward Burlingame/Harper & Row.

CHAPTER 2: A FRAMEWORK FOR PRINCIPAL LEADERSHIP

Bacharach, S.B., & Lawler, E.J. (1980). *Power and politics in organizations: The social psychology of conflict, coalitions, and bargaining.* San Francisco: Jossey-Bass.

Ball, S. (1987). *The micro-politics of the school: Toward a theory of school organization.* London: Methuen.

Berman, P., & McLaughlin, M.W. (1978). Federal programs supporting educational change: Vol. 8. Implementing and sustaining innovations. Santa Monica, CA: Rand Corporation.

Blase, J. (1989). The micro politics of the school: The everyday political perspective of teachers toward open school principals. *Educational Administration Quarterly, 24*(4), 377–407.

Crow, G.M. (1992). The principal in schools of choice. *The Urban Review, 24*(3).

Crow, G.M. (1990). Central office influence on the principal's relationship with teachers. *Administrators Notebook, 34*(1), 1–4.

Crow, G.M., & Slater, R.O. (1996). *Educating democracy: The role of systemic leadership.* Fairfax, VA: The National Policy Board for Educational Administration.

Deal, T.E., & Peterson, K.D. (1994). *The leadership paradox: Balancing logic and artistry in schools*. San Francisco: Jossey-Bass, Inc.

Duke, D.L. (1986). Aesthetics of leadership. *Educational Administration Quarterly, 22,* 7–27.

Foster, W.F. (1989). Toward a critical practice in leadership. In J. Smyth (Ed.). *Critical perspectives on educational leadership.* 39–62. London: Falmer.

Gabarro, J.J. (1974). Robert F. Kennedy High School. Case study. Cambridge, MA: Harvard University. (Distributed by Intercollegiate Case Clearing House, Soldiers Field, Boston, MA 02163).

Gamoran, A., & Dreeben, R. (1986). Coupling and control in educational organizations. *Administrative Science Quarterly, 31*(4), 612–632.

Hallinger, P., & Murphy, J. (1983). The social context of effective schools. *American Journal of Education, 94,* 328–355.

Hallinger, P., & Hausman, C. (1993). The changing role of the principal in a school of choice. In J. Murphy & P. Hallinger (Eds.). *Restructuring schooling. Learning from ongoing efforts.* 114–142. Newbury Park, CA: Corwin Press.

Hannaway, J., & Sproull, L. (1978). Who's running the show? Coordination and control in educational organizations. *Administrators Notebook, 27*(9), 1–4.

Hoyle, E. (1986). *The politics of school management.* London: Hodder and Stoughton.

Kelley, R.E. (1992). *The power of followership: How to create leaders people want to follow and followers who lead themselves.* New York: Doubleday.

Lieberman, A., & Miller, L. (1991). *Staff development for education in the 90s. New demands, new realities, new perspectives.* New York: Teachers College Press.

Little, J.W. (1982). Norms of collegiality and experimentation: Workplace conditions of school success. *American Educational Research Journal, 19,* 325–40.

Murphy, J., & Hallinger, P. (1993). *Restructuring schooling. Learning from ongoing efforts.* Newbury Park, CA: Corwin Press.

Peterson, K.D. (1984), Mechanisms of administrative control over managers in educational organizations. *Administrative Science Quarterly, 29,* 573–597.

Rost, J.C. (1991). *Leadership for the twenty-first century.* New York: Praeger.

Schlechty, P.C. (1990). *Schools for the twenty-first century. Leadership imperatives for educational reform.* San Francisco: Jossey-Bass.

Senge, P.M. (1990). The leader's new work: Building learning organizations. *MIT Sloan Management Review,* (Fall), 7–23.

Starratt, R.J. (1993). *The drama of leadership.* London: Falmer Press.

Thomson, S.D. (1993). *Principals for our changing schools. The knowledge and skill base.* Fairfax, VA: National Policy Board for Educational Administration.

Yukl, G. (1994). *Leadership in organizations, (3rd. ed.).* Englewood Cliffs, NJ: Prentice Hall.

CHAPTER 3: LEADERSHIP AND SCHOOL CULTURE: CREATING, MAINTAINING, AND CHANGING

Berliner, D.C., & Biddle, B.J. (1995). *The manufactured crisis: Myths, fraud, and the attack on America's public schools.* Reading, MA: Addison-Wesley.

Block, P. (1987). *The empowered manager.* San Francisco: Jossey-Bass.

Crow, G.M. (1994). Community and diversity: Administration in a democratic context. *NASSP Bulletin, 78*(558), 40–45.

Crow, G.M. (1993). Reconceptualizing the school administrator's role: Socialization at mid-career. *School Effectiveness and School Improvement, 4*(2), 131–152.

Daresh, J.C., & Playko, M.A. (1992). *The professional development of school administrators: Preservice, induction, and inservice applications.* Needham Heights, MA: Allyn and Bacon.

Deal, T.E., & Kennedy, A.A. (1982). *Corporate cultures: The rites and rituals of corporate life.* Reading, MA: Addison-Wesley

Deal, T.E., & Peterson, K.D. (1990). *The principal's role in shaping school culture.* Washington, DC: US Department of Education, Government Printing Office.

Dwyer, D. (1984). The search for instructional leadership: Routines and subtleties in the principal's role. *Educational Leadership, 41*(5).

Elam, S.M., & Rose, L.C. (1995). The 27th annual Phi Delta Kappa/Gallup poll of the public's attitudes toward the public school. *Phi Delta Kappan, 77,* 41–56.

Hart, A. W. (1993). *Principal succession: Establishing leadership in schools.* Albany, NY: State University of New York Press.

Hart, A.W., & Bredeson, P.V. (1996). *The principalship. A theory of professional learning and practice.* New York: McGraw-Hill.

Meyer, J.W. (1984). Organizations as ideological systems. In T.J. Sergiovanni and J.E. Corbally (Eds.) *Leadership and organizational culture. New perspectives on administrative theory and practice.* 186–206. Urbana, IL: University of Illinois Press.

Odden, A.R. (1995). *Educational leadership for American schools.* New York: McGraw-Hill.

Ott, J.S. (1989). *The organizational culture perspective.* Chicago: The Dorsey Press.

Peters, T.J., & Waterman, R.H., Jr. (1982). *In search of excellence: Lessons from America's best-run companies.* New York: Harper & Row.

Post, D. (1992). Through Joshua Gap: Curricular control and the constructed community. *Teachers College Press, 93*(4), 673–696.

Rost, J.C. (1991). *Leadership for the twenty-first century.* New York: Praeger.

Saphier, J., & King, M. (1985). Good seeds grow in strong cultures. *Educational Leadership, 42*(6), 67–74.

Schein, E.H. (1992). *Organizational culture and leadership.* (2nd ed). San Francisco: Jossey-Bass Publishers.

Schon, D.A. (1983). *The reflective practitioner: How professionals think in action.* New York: Basic Books.

Sergiovanni, T.J. (1995). *The principalship: A reflective practice perspective.* Boston: Allyn and Bacon.

Sergiovanni, T.J., & Corbally, J.E. (1984). *Leadership in organizational culture.* Urbana, IL: University of Illinois Press.

Weick, K. (1985). The significance of culture. In P.J. Frost et al. (Eds.) *Organizational culture.* Beverly Hills, CA: Sage Publications.

CHAPTER 4: INFLUENCING A COLLECTIVE VISION

Barth, R. (1986). The principal and the profession of teaching. *Elementary School Journal, 86*(4).

Brown, J.S. (1989). Remarks at a Stanford Center for Organizational Research Seminar, January 13, 1989.

Burns, J.M. (1978). *Leadership*. New York: Harper & Row.

Crow, G.M. (1992). The principal in schools of choice. *The Urban Review, 24*(3).

Crow, G.M., & Slater, R.O. (1996). *Educating democracy: The role of systemic leadership*. Fairfax, VA: The National Policy Board for Educational Administration.

Cuban, L. (1988). A fundamental puzzle of school reform. *Phi Delta Kappan, 69*(5), 340–344.

Dwyer, D. (1984). The search for instructional leadership: Routines and subtleties in the principal's role. *Educational Leadership, 41*(5).

Fullan, M.G. (1992). Vision that blinds. *Educational Leadership* (February), 19–20.

Mundez-Morse, S. (1995). Vision, leadership and change. Southwest Educational Development Laboratory, Leadership for Change Project.

Nanus, B. (1992). *Visionary leadership. Creating a compelling sense of direction for your organization*. San Francisco: Jossey-Bass.

Odden, A.R. (1995). *Educational leadership for American schools*. New York: McGraw-Hill.

Sashkin, M. (1988). The visionary leader. In J. Conger, R. Kanungo, et al., (Eds.), *Charismatic leadership. The elusive factor in organizational effectiveness*. San Francisco: Jossey-Bass.

Sergiovanni, T.J. (1995). *The principalship: A reflective practice perspective*. Boston: Allyn and Bacon.

Shekerjian, D. (1990). *Uncommon genius*. New York: Viking Penguin.

Sockett, H. (1987). Has Shulman got the strategy right? *Harvard Educational Review, 57*, 208–219.

Starratt, R.J. (1993). *The drama of leadership*. London: Falmer Press.

Starratt, R.J. (1996). *Transforming educational administration: Meaning, community and excellence*. New York: McGraw-Hill.

Vaill, P.B., (1984). The purpose of high performing systems. In T.J. Sergiovanni and J.E. Corbally (Eds.) *Leadership and organizational culture: New perspectives on administrative theory and practice*. Urbana, IL: University of Illinois Press.

Weick, K. (1978). The spines of leaders. In M.W. McCall, Jr., and M. M. Lombardo (Eds.). *Leadership: Where else can we go?* 37–61. Durham, NC: Duke University.

Westley, F.R., & Mintzberg, H. (1988). Profiles of strategic vision: Levesque and Iacocca. In J.A. Conger et al. (Eds.). *Charismatic leadership. The elusive factor in organizational effectiveness*. 161–212. San Francisco: Jossey-Bass.

CHAPTER 5: LEADERSHIP FOR SCHOOL IMPROVEMENT: INFLUENCING AN ENVIRONMENT FOR CHANGE

Bellah, R.N., Madsen, R., Sullivan, W.M., Swidler, A., & Tipton, S.M. (1985). *Habits of the heart*. New York: Harper & Row.

Berman, P., & McLaughlin, M.W. (1978). Federal programs supporting educational change: Vol. 8. Implementing and sustaining innovations. Santa Monica, CA: Rand Corporation.

Burns, J. M. (1978). *Leadership*. New York: Harper & Row.

Crow, G.M., & Slater, R.O. (1996). *Educating democracy: The role of systemic leadership*. Fairfax, VA: The National Policy Board for Educational Administration.

Dewey, J. (1900). *The school and the society*. Chicago, University of Chicago Press.

Firestone, W.A., & Corbett, H.D. (1988). Planned organizational change. In N.J. Boyan (Ed.), *Handbook of research on educational administration*. 32–340. New York: Longman.

Fullan, M.G. (1992). *Successful school improvement. The implementation perspective and beyond*. Philadelphia: Open University Press.

Hart, A.W. (1993). A design studio for reflective practice. In P. Hallinger, E. Leithwood, and J. Murphy (Eds.). *Cognitive perspectives on educational leadership*. New York: Teachers College Press.

Heller, M.F. & Firestone, W.A. (1995). Who's in charge here? Sources of leadership for change in eight schools. *Elementary School Journal*, 96(1), 65–86.

Kanter, R.M. (1983). *The change masters. Innovation for productivity in the American corporation.* New York: Simon and Schuster.

Kouzes, J.M., & Posner, B.Z. (1987). *The leadership challenge. How to get extraordinary things done in organizations.* San Francisco: Jossey-Bass.

Lortie, D.C. (1975). *Schoolteacher: A sociological study.* Chicago: University of Chicago Press.

Osterman, K.F., & Kottkamp, R.B. (1993). *Reflective practice for educators. Improving schooling through professional development.* Newbury Park, CA: Corwin Press.

Rost, J.C. (1991). *Leadership for the twenty-first century.* New York: Praeger.

Senge, P.M. (1990). The leader's new work: Building learning organizations. *MIT Sloan Management Review,* (Feb.), 7–23.

Starratt, R.J. (1996). *Transforming educational administration: Meaning, community and excellence.* New York: McGraw-Hill.

Teddlie, C., & Stringfield, S. (1993). *Schools make a difference. Lessons learned form a 10-year study of school effects.* New York: Teachers College.

CHAPTER 6: A LEADERSHIP ROLE FOR PRINCIPALS: REALISTIC AND RELEVANT

Burns, J. M. (1978). *Leadership.* New York: Harper and Row.

Crow, G.M., & Slater, R.O. (1996). *Educating democracy: The role of systemic leadership.* Fairfax, VA: The National Policy Board for Educational Administration.

Odden, A.R. (1995). *Educational leadership for American schools.* New York: McGraw-Hill.

Rost, J.C. (1991). *Leadership for the twenty-first century.* New York: Praeger

Schlechty, P.C. (1990). *Schools for the twenty-first century. Leadership imperatives for educational reform.* San Francisco: Jossey-Bass.